W9-CNL-525

Contents

SLOWINGDOWN THE AGING PROCESS

●

HANS J. KUGLER, Ph.D.

PYRAMID BOOKS ● *NEW YORK*

SLOWING DOWN THE AGING PROCESS

A PYRAMID BOOK

Second printing March, 1974

ISBN 0-515-03099-6

Library of Congress Catalog Card Number: 74-61

Copyright © 1973 by Hans J. Kugler, Ph.D.
All Rights Reserved

Pyramid Books are published by Pyramid Communications, Inc. Its trademarks, consisting of the word "Pyramid" and the portrayal of a pyramid, are registered in the United States Patent Office.

Printed in the United States of America

PYRAMID COMMUNICATIONS, INC.
919 Third Avenue
New York, New York 10022, U.S.A.

HERE IS THE BOOK

that tells all about aging in fascinating, critical detail—the facts and the fictions about a subject that concerns every one of us:

- *the biology, physiology and psychology of aging*
- the relationship of exercise and proper *nutrition* to a long, healthy life
- a close look at the *Stillman, Solomon and Atkins* diets
- *tension, smoking, air pollution*—and your health
- *youth surgery and drugs*
- *cell therapy and Regeneresen*
- *cryonics* (deep freezing and "super-cooling")
- *organic foods and vitamins*—how necessary are they?
- *QUIZ: How high is your risk of aging prematurely?*

Yes, YOU CAN LIVE A HAPPIER, LONGER LIFE . . .

Here's why—and here's how!

DR. HANS J. KUGLER was born in Germany and attended the University of Munich, where he studied under Nobel Prize winner A. Butenandt. He received his Doctorate in chemistry from State University of New York at Stony Brook in 1967. He is presently teaching and engaged in gerontology research at Roosevelt University in Chicago. His other publications include articles in various scientific and chemical journals.

For valuable contributions and/or discussions, I would like to express my thanks to:

Prof. H. Hoepke, M.D., Heidelberg, Germany, expert on cell therapy.

Prof. D. F. Chebotarev, director of the Russian institute of gerontology.

Benjamin S. Frank, M.D., originator of the nucleic acid therapy.

Prof. G. Orzechowski, M.D., Cologne, Germany, expert on injectable organ-specific nucleic acids.

Dr. Richard A. Passwater, Silver Springs, Maryland, consultant in gerontology.

Prof. Hans Selye, University of Montreal.

and to
"Munschie."

I would also like to express my thanks to:

Dr. M. Srinivassen, University of Illinois, Medical Center, for a discussion on sex and older people; and

S. Felix, M.D., plastic surgeon, River Forest, Illinois, for a discussion on youth surgery; and Mr. B. Krozel and Miss Jeanne Eggers, Chicago, for editing parts of this book.

The views expressed in this book are not necessarily the views of the researchers mentioned above.

Introduction

It is a very natural feeling that you should want to stay young-looking, physically fit, and mentally alert for the longest time possible. This book attempts to synthesize the available scientific data and to help you obtain this goal.

I have surveyed approximately 1000 persons, mostly young people in colleges and a few old persons. I asked them a number of questions that I thought every person concerned with his health should be able to answer.

Here are the questions:

(1) What do you know about nutrition? (2) Are you jeopardizing your health by smoking cigarettes? (3) What happens when you smoke a cigarette? (4) Does exercise make you live longer? (5) Does it improve your sex life? (6) Does it make your system more resistent to disease? (7) Do you know any ways to slow down premature aging? (8) What do you have to do if you want to live longer? (9) Does an active sex life cut down on your average life expectancy? (10) What is aging? (11) Do scientists have ways to slow it down?

The answers I received on these questions led me to one conclusion: NOBODY KNEW ANYTHING! Since I have been teaching in college for several years, I would like to draw an anology from my experience as an educator to explain the reason for this profound lack of knowledge about aging. When you teach a college level course, you first have to evaluate how much information the average student can digest. You can cover in class only a certain amount of specially selected materials. While you do this, you also have to point out to the student the most important facts, emphasizing and deemphasizing certain information, yet making sure that the average student gets the whole picture. In other words, you have to "predigest" the material before you feed it to the student and, from time to time, repeat the most important ideas. But if you overburden the students with 5 to 10 times the material they can handle, you will only confuse them; they will not recognize what is important and your efforts will prove to be a waste of time.

With the large variety of literature available on health and aging, your dilemma is very similar to the over-burdened college student. The majority of books and scientific papers on aging cover only special areas of study and don't attempt to correlate it with other important areas.

In many instances this literature is written primarily for professionals. Some authors pick up good ideas that would interest the public but after the first few pages, they become so technical that the average reader is unable to understand what they have to say.

During the last two and one-half years I have read and evaluated more than 800 scientific papers and books in the health and aging field. A summary of this material would take at least 2000 pages and *would* probably overwhelm even the most determined reader. But who wants to read a summary? You want to know in as few pages as possible what science can do to slow down the aging process, which methods work, and what you can do this very moment with your body. I have evaluated my readings in a direct and matter-of-fact manner. The book might at times read a little telegraphically, but I think that this is better than making a falsely dramatic story out of information that should be looked at with a clear and objective mind.

I have tried to answer the questions that an inquisitive person might have. For instance, what is aging and what are the major causes of aging? Which elements and chemicals in the body affect the aging process? Do proteins, carbohydrates, fats, vitamins, minerals, and enzymes have any special effect on the aging process? Is it important to cut down on smoking, to exercise, to breathe clean air? Does sex make one age faster? Are scientists solving the aging problem? Is it possible to prolong my life expectancy? Which chemicals do scientists use to slow down the aging process? What can I do to prevent arteriosclerosis and heart attack? Is it possible to reverse or stop the aging process? Can my doctor help me?

As a factual report on all the different ways scientists and doctors are trying to slow down the aging process, this book can help you understand more about how to stay young looking, physically fit, and mentally alert. Besides it also provides you with a simple, handy reference to all the complex and varied areas of research in the field of health and aging.

ABOUT ADVICE: As we discuss the different areas of aging in the following chapters I will often give you advice and ask you to do some additional reading in other fields. Since you want to make sure that you get the best advice, I believe you should be extremely critical in determining to whom you want to listen.

If you decide to do some additional reading on nutrition, make sure that the author has a good background in biochemistry or nutrition. A Medical Doctor alone is not good enough as I will explain later. And a health nut who just read a lot about nutrition is an absolute NO-NO. If you want to go on a diet to lose weight, this is even more important because many

11

"diet-experts" (including some doctors) give absolutely wrong advice. If the person who works out a diet for you is fat himself, forget him. Does somebody advise you on health with a cigarette in his (or her) hand? Don't waste your money. Does whoever is working out an exercise program for you have a pot belly and takes an elevator to go up to the second floor? Find yourself another advisor. If somebody advises you on stress and takes medicine for ulcers, don't listen to him!

We don't really know exactly what causes aging but there are enough research results available that show that an average life expectancy of at least 110 years, while staying physically fit and mentally alert, is definitely possible. Since you are probably very anxious to slow down your aging process or prevent premature aging, here are a few rules that you can follow right now.

Get a physical from your doctor and ask him if there is any reason why you should not follow any of the following advice:

Cut down on your carbohydrate and fat intake. Eat more (and different) types of proteins. Drink a glass of multi-vegetable juice every day. Eat more fish, rice and some caviar. Take a good multivitamin and some extra vitamin E and C and 2 teaspoons of safflower oil every day. Drink one glass of water with every meal. Don't go on any one of the quick weight loss diets.

Start a light exercise program. Any exercise is good, but jogging is best. If you have not done any exercise recently, start very slowly and build up. For example, if you want to start jogging, start walking at an accelerated pace first and after one or two weeks start jogging about two times, one or two minutes per day and build up very slowly.

Evaluate your stress situation. Learn about stress

and how to cope with it. Even if you can't change your stress situation, knowing how to deal with it can help a lot. If your stress situation is serious, read *The Stress of Life* by Hans Selye.

If you smoke, prepare yourself to quit smoking by cutting down on the number of cigarettes smoked and by smoking only half the cigarette. Convince yourself that smoking has only negative effects on your health. DO ANYTHING THAT WILL HELP YOU QUIT SMOKING.

And now, since you have a good start, relax, sit down and read about all the ways to slow down aging so that you can add years to your life and life to your years.

PART I

Aging is an Unnecessary Evil

Despite all the research results in human aging we have merely scratched the surface. The time has come, however, when we can evaluate these results and draw many important conclusions.

Several causes of aging, and especially premature aging, are already known but not yet 100% proven. Still, these research results suggest many possible ways to slow down the aging process. And what is even more important, the methods suggested here certainly wouldn't do any harm even if some of them should be proven wrong or unnecessary later.

CHAPTER 1

To Age or Not to Age,

That Is the Question

Our goals: To stay physically fit, mentally alert and young-looking into a much older age; and to lengthen our life span by slowing down the aging process.

Throughout history man has been searching for the Fountain of Youth or other mystical remedies to achieve eternal youth. In comparison with the slow evolution of knowledge in nonscientific areas of study, not much time has passed between the medieval wizard who mixed mysterious potions in his crude laboratory and today's modern biochemist who investigates life processes with the most advanced equipment. Yet science is at the doorstep of discovering the origins of life and the processes that cause aging.

The present goal of a large number of serious scientists is to find reliable ways to keep man physically fit and mentally alert into an older age and to slow down and even to stop the aging process. Some researchers talk about the possibility of prolonging the human life span to 300 years. Believe it or not, there is already some experimental evidence that this is possible. I personally believe that in the near future man will be able to extend his life span 30 to 50 years by simply taking a daily pill. I also believe that he will be able to stay physically fit and mentally alert for both his daily and nightly tasks. Actually my projections are conservative in light of information that is available on this subject. Since many theories have been proposed to explain the human aging process, I have selected those that are, in my opinion, the most important and are supported by a number of concurrent scientific results. The less known theories will not be ignored but mentioned in relation to their importance.

I am repeatedly asked by interested friends: What does "prolonging our life span" actually mean? Will we still grow old and just stay alive for these extra years or can we look and stay younger for a longer time? The answer is simple. Your average life expectancy is, at present, 70 years. If you could expand your life expectancy to 140 years, your aging process would be spread (prolonged) over a period of 140 years. This means that a person of 70 years would look as young as a person of 35. Many laboratory experiments are now being conducted to find ways to keep people looking and feeling young for 70 or 80% of their total life span.

It is likely that you have, at one time or another, picked up a biology or psychology book that contains statistical data on all the important changes in the life cycle of the "average human being." You are amazed to learn that if you are more than 25 years old, you have already passed the point of your maximum performance and efficiency and that your health is going downhill at a tremendous rate. But do you bother to ask yourself who this "average human being" is? If someone shows you statistical information indicating that persons 70 years of age are senile, do you believe that you too will be senile when you reach the age of 70?

It is important then, to take a *new* look at yourself. On the following page, I have drawn performance and efficiency curves that will show you what you can do for yourself if you (1) live and act in accord with some of the latest research results and (2) are reason-

18

Figure 1.

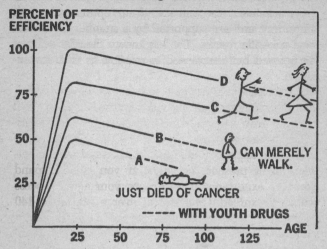

able and "listen" to your body's requests to treat it differently. Figure 1 shows estimated performance curves of different persons. Which description fits you? Think positively! Research in biochemistry has advanced at a tremendous rate. Just recently, new scientific theories on the aging process have emerged like supernovae in the sky, and experimental proof for these theories looks excellent.

Actually most of us (often unknowingly) behave like idiots—asking for trouble by continuing with our present life styles. But don't be alarmed, you do not necessarily have to make any drastic changes in your life style in order to improve. You have to know the proper foods and food supplements and develop a steady rest pattern. You must also exercise and possess a basic knowledge of certain drugs. If you can master these basic principles, in all likelihood you can improve your physical and mental alertness tremendously and maybe keep yourself fit *up* to an age of 90 or 100. And this is just the beginning. As I said earlier, sooner or later (research indicates that it will be sooner) it will be possible to slow down the aging process by merely taking a daily pill.

I'm sure that you are asking yourself: How many years can I add to my life expectancy if I would change one or another of my habits? I want to give you the facts that will let you know which factors contribute to aging. If you can understand the problem, you will be more willing to accept the "do's and don'ts" in the following chapters.

The human body is like a big test tube with thousands of different reactions continuously going on inside it. The exploration of the aging process is comparable to studying a chemical reaction taking place in a test tube. Once the path (or mechanism) of the reaction is known, it is much easier to interfere with it, slow it down, or accelerate it or stop it completely. This is what scientists are now trying to do with the aging processes taking place within the human body.

Several companies already have patents, patent applications or even manufactured drugs (I call them youth compounds) that are supposed to slow down the aging process or prolong the average life expectancy (2). With one of these geriatric drugs, organ specific nucleic acids, I obtained some good results on test animals in my own laboratory. Actually many of these drugs have no "secret" ingredients at all and it is already possible to add to your daily diet a number of chemical compounds which contain concentrations of the basic ingredients of these new drugs. I will explain more about these new "youth" drugs in Chapters 5, 6, 11, 15 and 19.

One last note. Every chapter has its importance and contributes to the understanding of the aging processes. You simply cannot attribute health and long life to any one type of improvement, as has been done so many times before. While improvement in one specific area is good for *that* area, *overall* improvement is then not too impressive. Remember: If you want to extend your life expectancy, you also want to make sure that you can enjoy those extra years.

Figure 2.

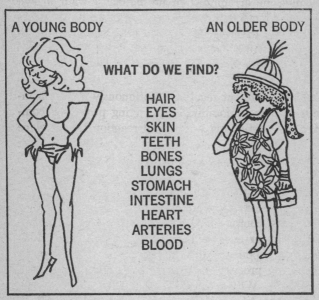

A YOUNG BODY   AN OLDER BODY

WHAT DO WE FIND?

HAIR
EYES
SKIN
TEETH
BONES
LUNGS
STOMACH
INTESTINE
HEART
ARTERIES
BLOOD

CHAPTER 2

Aging and the Single Cell

YOUTH: Newly formed cells in our body out-
number dying cells. This constitutes the growth
period.
ADULTHOOD: The number of dying cells is
balanced by new cells.
AGING: Fewer new cells are formed than cells
that die. Aging is a constant loss of cells.

It is possible to describe the physical changes of a human as he ages in terms of his posture, skin, eyes, hair, muscle tone, bone structure, etc. But a mere description doesn't explain the aging process. Where does aging start? What parts of the body ages? Muscles, skeleton, collagen (connective tissue), nerves, etc. However, in order to make valid observations you have to examine all types of tissues with a microscope. You will then find that every kind of tissue has, as its smallest unit, the cell.

About 100 years ago Matthias Schwann and Theodor Schweiden recognized that the cell is the fundamental unit of all living organisms. Millions of cells make up your skin and your muscles. No matter which organism you examine, you will always find that it is composed of cells. When cells get worn out they divide and form new cells. All the basic biochemical processes take place or begin in the cell. However, old cells that have gone through many cell divisions do not perform these biochemical operations as well as young cells. In the first stages of life (up to age 18) there is an excessive formation of new cells which constitutes the growth period. During early adulthood (18-25 years of age), newly formed cells balance the number of dying cells. When aging sets in, more cells die than are formed.

The formation of life starts with a single cell which, when fertilized, starts dividing and multiplying to

Figure 3.

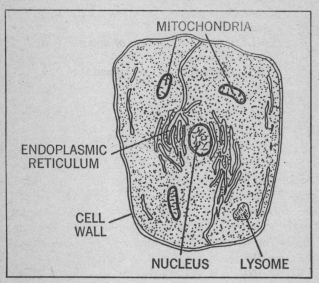

form the human embryo. Figure 3 shows the basic structure of a cell. Even though muscle cells are different from nerve cells, which are in turn different from structural cells, they all contain the same basic units—cell membrane, cytoplasm, and nucleus.

The three most important small organs (organelles) are contained in the cytoplasm. These organelles are (1) *Endoplasmic Reticulum,* which is the site of protein synthesis and possibly also serves for exchange of metabolites. (2) *Mitochondria,* the energy converters of your cells which, for example, show the conversion (oxidation) of sugar to energy and then store it in the form of high energy molecules called ATP (adenosinetriphosphate); and (3) *Lysomes,* which contain enzymes that break down larger molecules into smaller molecules for other processes in the cell.

The nucleus of the cell contains chromosomes. The basic structure of the chromosomes is DNA (deoxiribonucleic acid). All the hereditary information and the instructions for every biochemical process in the living cell are precisely coded on this DNA molecule. Think of DNA as the "central director" of all life processes.

When J. Watson and F. Crick at Cambridge University discovered the structure of DNA, they were only a fraction of an inch from the discovery of the secret of life. They discovered that the DNA molecule consists of two strands of sugar and phosphate molecules which are held together by four substances called bases. The frequency and sequence of these four recurring bases constitute the DNA code. The whole DNA molecule is coiled like a double helix.

Figure 4 shows a small section of the DNA molecule. When a cell divides to form new cells the DNA molecule uncoils, separates down the middle, and each half of the DNA replicates its other half again. There are then two complete DNAs which become the nucleus of a new cell. The original cell is now divided and has formed two new DNAs.

How does the DNA control the functions of the cell? I pointed out earlier that all the biochemical processes in the cell are directed by DNA. Let's assume that somewhere in the cell the synthesis (or production) of a protein is required. How can the DNA, confined in the nucleus, direct the synthesis of a protein in another part of the cell? Two compounds, Messen-

Figure 4.

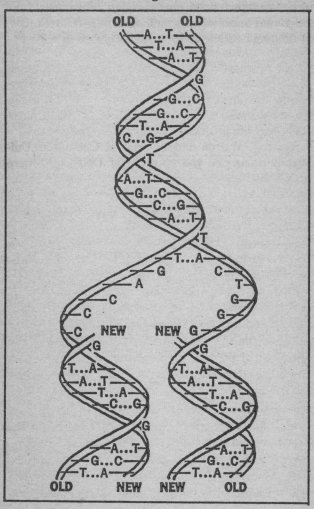

ger RNA and Transfer RNA are involved. When DNA begins issuing its directions, a Messenger RNA is formed automatically and receives from the DNA an exact set of instructions to form the new protein. The Messenger RNA then travels to the site where the formation of the protein is required. With the help of Transfer RNA (which supplies the basic chemicals), the synthesis of the new protein takes place.

Why is it important to keep your cells in good health? When a cell wears out it divides automatically and forms two new cells. Why then, should you worry about your cells if new cells are being manufactured? Shouldn't you need to supply your body with the right nutrients and assume that any damage will be repaired by the new cells? NO. For two reasons: (1) As mentioned earlier, cells that have gone through many divisions perform their duties less efficiently and (2) more importantly, there are only a limited number of cell divisions available. Professor L. Hayflick at the University of Stanford isolated cells from the human embryo and allowed them to live and divide in an inert medium; they divided approximately 50 times and died. Cells from persons between one and 20 years of age divided approximately 30 times and died (3). This suggests a limited life span. Therefore, in order to prolong your life span, you have to protect your cells from wearing out. Several researchers have been quite critical about this concept of finite cell divisions (144, 145, 146).

We have several kinds of extremely important cells in our body that don't divide—brain cells, for example. I believe that there is enough evidence that the final death of a species is caused by an increasing death of nondividing cells of major organs. That means when a critical number of cells of a major organ have died, it causes the collapse of the entire organ which in turn causes the organ system to cease its functions and so on.

It is therefore of the utmost importance to supply our cells with optimum conditions at all times in order to keep them alive for the longest time possible.

CHAPTER 3

Important Aging Factors

Evaluations of available data suggest that the maximum possible life span for the species man is approximately 120 to 130 years. The goal of many researchers is to extend our life expectancy past these 130 years. Our first steps, however, should be directed towards increasing the efficiency of our entire system so that our performance at age 80 is not much lower than it was at age 40. We already know how to do this.

Aging is a constant loss of cells. That's a fact well agreed on by the experts. But the question "why do we lose cells" is difficult to answer. Scientists know that aging is not caused by one single factor; instead, it is an extremely complex process. But there is hope. For two reasons: (1) You don't have to solve the entire problem in order to lengthen your life span; and (2) several factors that cause or at least contribute to aging are already known. (See Figure 5 for a summary.)

The major factors that cause the destruction of cells are (1) the damage of the DNA, the central director of all cell functions, (2) an increase in large molecules due to cross-linking of smaller molecules and (3) a constant decrease in the effectiveness of all cell functions due to "stress." Factors that wear out your cells and drive them to the point where they divide too early are faulty nutrition, smoking, lack of exercise, air pollution and emotional stress in general.

Figure 5.

AGING IS A CONSTANT LOSS OF CELLS. WE LOSE CELLS BECAUSE

the efficiency of the cell is decreased due to toxic chemicals which interfere with metabolic processes (air pollution, smoking, alcohol, certain food preservatives, drugs etc.).

the cell wall and the organelles are constantly damaged by radicals. Radicals are formed due to the effects of radiation, air pollution, and faulty nutrition.

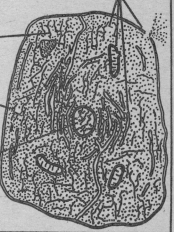

cross-linking forms large molecules which clog up the entire system (radicals, oxidation products, metal ions and other cross-linkers).

the DNA in the nucleus is damaged by cross-linking and by radicals.

the lack of the right nutrients hampers the metabolic processes.

Since many excellent reviews and books have already been written about these topics, I have covered only the basic and most important facts.

Of the three major causes of cell destruction, damage to DNA is the most serious. Two theories deal with DNA damage: The "somatic" theory and the newer, precise and factual theory of Dr. H. J. Curtis of the Brookhaven National Laboratory (135). Dr. Curtis has worked in aging research for many years and published some of the most interesting research results. Among other things, the increasing chromosome aberrations which occur with age were measured. Radiation also induces chromosome damage, but the life-shortening effect due to radiation is not directly proportional to the chromosome damage and amount of radiation. After a high dosage of radiation, the chromosome aberrations were high, but returned to the values of the control within a short time span. It was therefore necessary to assume that the increased rate of degenerative diseases due to radiation must involve several steps (136,137,138). All these findings suggest that chromosome damage is one, but not the only cause of aging.

Other ways to change chromosomes and with this the effect of chromosomes on aging were discovered by H. von Hahn in Switzerland. Dr. Hahn studied a group of compounds associated with the DNA, called histones. It was discovered that these histones cling more strongly to the DNA in old age. Thus, old DNA could be somewhat inhibited in its normal functions. One way to explain this could be that the histones are attached to the DNA via cross-links.

But there are still other ways a DNA can be damaged and lose its gene coding. B. L. Strehler and R. Johnson recently discussed the possibility of some kind of gene-slippage (141). Let us represent the DNA molecule here as Figure 6:

Figure 6.

```
SLIPPAGE
 — A — C — A — T — G — T — G — G — A —
   ))  ))  ))  ))  ))  ))  ))  ))  ))
→— T — G — T — A — C — A — C — C — T —→
```

If a slippage of one strand, via loop formation or otherwise, occurs, we have an altered DNA molecule (Figure 7):

```
 — A — C — A — T — G — T — G — G — A —
   ))  ))  ))  ))  ))  ))  ))  ))  ))  ))
     — T — G — T — A — C — A — C — C — T —
```

Figure 7.

Obviously, if the top DNA had the correct gene coding, the changed DNA would carry and pass on the wrong information.

Professor Strehler is one of the leading researchers in gerontology and works at the University of Southern California in Los Angeles.

Two other important research results were disclosed by H. J. Curtis et al. at the Annual Meeting of The Gerontological Society in December 1972. The first one is that chromosome aberrations occur with increasing temperatures (142). And the second one was the finding that chromosome aberrations occurred at about the same rate in long-lived as in short-lived mice when irradiated with gamma rays (143). This result suggests that the importance of the DNA repair mechanism in aging is somewhat overemphasized.

And now let's answer the question why a damaged DNA can be so effectively life-terminating.

DNA controls every biochemical process that takes place in the cell. The basic building blocks of the DNA molecule are called nucleotides. Nucleotides, in groups of three, pass on one unit of information, and each DNA molecule contains approximately 4,800,-000,000 nucleotides. (It's like having that many different words to describe one human being.) If for any reason a nucleotide is damaged and not repaired immediately, its damaged properties are carried over into another cell.

Let's now start with a young, perfect DNA (Figure 8). Part of it is represented by a long chain of letters A, T, C, and G. The same letters are used in biochemistry because the four bases in the DNA are Adenine, Thymine, Cytosine, and Guanine. During the first stage of life, damage can occur to the DNA molecule through a variety of reactions. It is also possible that mistakes are transmitted when the cell divides. When an error is carried over to the next DNA,

Figure 8.

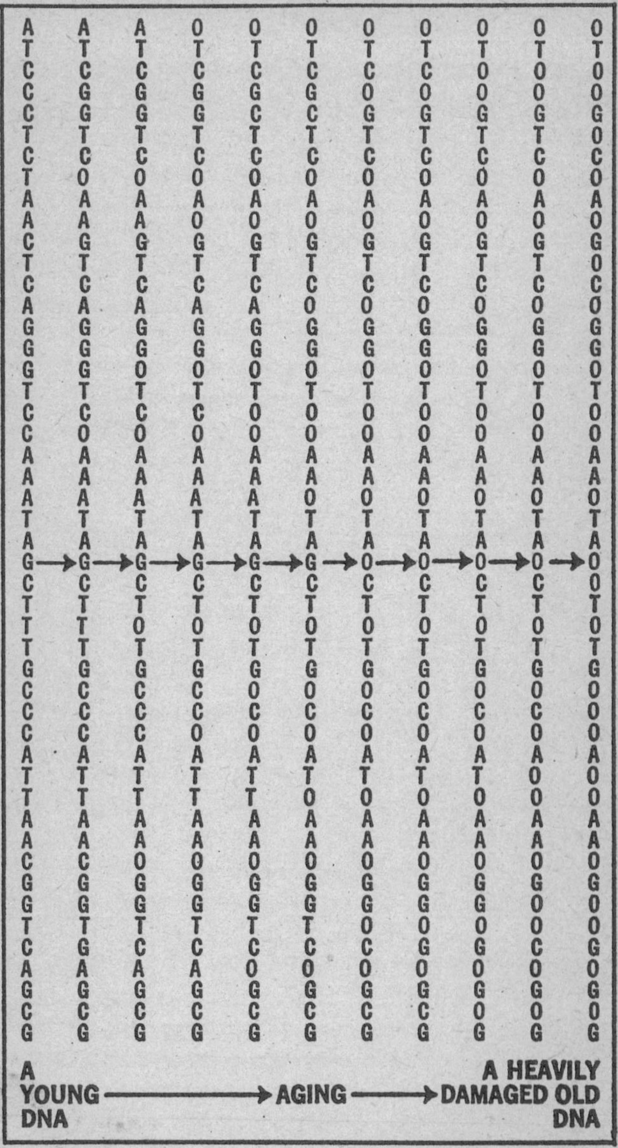

```
A  A  A  O  O  O  O  O  O  O  O
T  T  T  T  T  T  T  T  O  O  O
C  C  C  C  C  C  C  C  C  O  O
C  G  G  G  G  G  G  G  G  G  O
C  T  T  T  T  T  T  T  T  T  O
T  C  C  C  C  C  C  C  C  C  O
C  O  O  O  O  O  O  O  O  O  O
T  A  A  A  A  A  A  A  A  A  A
A  A  A  O  O  O  O  O  O  O  O
A  G  G  G  G  G  G  G  G  G  G
C  T  T  T  T  T  T  T  T  T  T
T  C  C  C  C  C  C  C  C  C  C
C  A  A  A  A  O  O  O  O  O  O
A  G  G  G  G  G  G  G  G  G  G
G  G  G  G  G  O  O  O  O  O  O
G  G  G  G  G  G  G  G  G  O  O
G  T  T  T  T  T  T  T  T  T  O
T  C  C  C  C  O  O  O  O  O  O
C  C  C  C  O  O  O  O  O  O  O
C  O  O  O  O  O  O  O  O  O  O
A  A  A  A  A  A  A  A  A  A  A
A  A  A  A  A  A  A  A  A  A  A
A  A  A  A  O  O  O  O  O  O  O
T  T  T  T  T  T  T  T  T  T  O
A  A  A  A  A  A  A  A  A  A  A
T  T  T  T  T  O  O  O  O  O  O
A  A  A  A  A  A  A  A  A  A  A
G→ G→ G→ G→ G→ O→ O→ O→ O→ O→ O
C  C  C  C  C  C  C  C  C  C  O
T  T  T  T  T  T  T  T  T  T  T
T  T  O  O  O  O  O  O  O  O  O
T  T  T  T  T  T  T  T  T  T  T
G  G  G  G  G  G  G  G  G  G  G
C  C  C  C  O  O  O  O  O  O  O
C  C  C  O  O  O  O  O  O  O  O
C  C  C  C  O  O  O  O  O  O  O
A  A  A  A  A  A  A  A  A  A  A
T  T  T  T  T  T  T  T  T  T  O
T  T  T  T  O  O  O  O  O  O  O
A  A  A  A  A  A  A  A  A  A  A
A  A  A  A  A  A  A  A  A  A  A
C  C  C  C  C  C  C  C  C  C  C
G  G  G  G  G  G  G  G  G  G  G
G  G  G  G  G  G  G  G  G  G  G
T  T  T  T  T  O  O  O  O  O  O
C  C  C  C  C  C  C  C  C  C  C
A  A  A  A  O  O  O  O  O  O  O
G  G  G  G  G  G  G  G  G  G  G
C  C  C  C  C  C  C  C  O  O  O
G  G  G  G  G  G  G  G  G  O  G
G  G  G  G  G  G  G  G     G  G
```

A YOUNG DNA ——————→ AGING ——————→ A HEAVILY DAMAGED OLD DNA

it will not be very significant at first. After many cell divisions, however, the difference between the first and the last DNA becomes remarkable. Eventually the damage becomes so serious that the performance of the DNA becomes completely unsatisfactory and ceases to function. Such a change is represented in Figure 8: When a nucleotide is damaged, it is changed from a letter to circle to indicate the damage.

Let's assume now that part of the DNA depicted in Figure 8 is responsible for the synthesis of an enzyme. The young DNA will then pass on a perfect set of instructions for the synthesis of a well-functioning enzyme. However, a DNA that has gone through six cell divisions might produce an enzyme that still works fairly well, even though it already contains several mistakes in its structure.

An old DNA (the last column in Figure 8) will, without doubt, be unable to produce a normal functioning enzyme. Inactive enzymes obviously formed from damaged DNAs were detected in old organisms.

It is also known that the RNA in your cells decrease after the age of 40. Therefore some researchers believe that the decreased formation of proteins or enzymes is due to a lack of or damage to RNA. But why does the RNA decrease in older age? Isn't it more reasonable to assume that the decreased amounts of RNA are due to damaged or otherwise changed DNA since the DNA is responsible for the RNA formation in the first place?

Even if aging was proven to result from changed DNA, that still wouldn't satisfy a biochemist. He has to go a step further. The next question is: Why did the DNA change?

If there was a sudden decrease in the population of the country, the scientist certainly wouldn't stop his inquiry once he had determined a certain illness might have caused the decrease. Naturally

33

to find out which virus or bacteria caused the illness. Only after he has determined this will he be able to find a cure for the disease. In aging research, it's a little bit like that but much more complicated since the entire aging process is due to a large number of causes.

The second cause for the over-all decreased efficiency of your system with age, which also contributes to the loss of cells, is a constantly increasing number of large molecules throughout your body. These large molecules clog up your system and interfere with the biochemical processes in your cells. The number of these large molecules increases with age. This also constitutes aging and is discussed in detail in Chapter 6.

Many theories on aging describe the changes that occur in your body during the aging process, but only a few of them explain the reason for these changes; even fewer can prove that their suggested cause actually produces the change. Therefore two theories that were able to do both will get some special attention. "The Free Radical Theory" and the "Cross-Link Theory" are actually very closely related and will be discussed in detail in Chapters 5 and 6.

If you could prevent only 10% of the aging factors in your system and un-do another 10% of the damage already done, your maximum life expectancy would be approximately 280 to 340 years. But it is unnecessary to solve the entire aging problem to increase your average life expectancy. If science could solve th̄e ēntire aging problem, you could stop aging com-

lready convincing evidence from labora-
ts on test animals that the aging proc-
OWED DOWN. By feeding mice a
t nutrients, Vitamin E, sulfur ami-
dants, it was possible to extend

34

the average life expectancy of these test animals 166% (1). These results are fantastic and represent a break-through in aging research.

Here I am talking about prolonging your life span. But there are still several diseases that can terminate your life before you have a chance to get old—such as cancer. Even though a lot of work is being done in this area, scientists haven't yet discovered the cure. However, cancer cells, if detected early enough, can be cut out or killed by radiation, freezing, or drugs. It is pretty well established that cancer is linked to viruses. Viruses are extremely small; and once they infect a cell, they trigger the cell division mechanism and the uncontrollable cancer growth starts (86, 87). There is also evidence that very reactive molecules, called free radicals, are somehow involved in cancer formation (147). Researchers are exploring every area for a cancer cure. There are many drugs that look promising, but many scientists feel that it might be better to use the genetic mechanism of the cells them-selves to stop the cancer growth.

An important finding that emphasizes the impor-tance of cancer prevention comes from the University of California. Dr. M. Baluda has found evidence that the basic information for the formation of cancer vi-ruses is carried by your genes (88). Therefore you should be extremely careful not to activate these genes and thus start the formation of the viruses. Smoking is one of those carcinogens (cancer activa-tors).

Other research results that emphasize the impor-tance of cancer prevention come from the area of an-tioxidants. Dr. Passwater at the American Gerontolog-ical Laboratory has observed that cancer in test ani-mals can drastically be reduced by using antioxidants like vitamin E, C, BHT, selenium, and sulfur amino acids (148). R. J. Shamberger and G. Rudolph have

35

also demonstrated on test animals that carcinogenesis can be prevented by the use of antioxidants (121, 122). W. Jaffe found that rats that were fed a diet which contained wheat germ oil had a smaller number of tumors after they were treated with a powerful tumor-causing chemical, 3-methylcholanthrene (123). S. Haber and R. Wissler injected mice with methylcholanthrene and found that a diet containing vitamin E had a highly inhibitory effect on the cancer formation in these animals (124). R. J. Shamberger demonstrated in a recent paper that there is a definite relationship between the decrease of gastric cancer in humans in this country and the use of antioxidants like BHT and BHA. He also showed that there was a definite decrease in the death rate from stomach cancer where people were taking in higher quantities of selenium (125).

But don't make the assumption that you protect yourself from lung cancer, if you are a heavy smoker, by taking antioxidants like vitamin E. Smoking cigarettes seems to be such a strong carcinogenic that even the strongest antioxidants cannot prevent it. Your only hope is to quit.

Cigarette smokers have a very high incidence of bladder cancer. This is because a compound called 3-hydroxyanthranilic acid is converted into the carcinogen cinnabaric acid in the urine. In the presence of antioxidants like vitamin C, this conversion does not happen. Thus, vitamin C might protect cigarette smokers from bladder cancer (148).

Sputum cytology is a new method for the earliest possible lung cancer detection; it will be discussed in Chapter 16. To protect your healthy cells from being damaged is of the utmost importance since you personally can do little to cure diseased cells. But you can take simple precautions to keep your cells healthy and to prolong your life.

Here then are the six major steps to stay younger for a longer time:

(1) You can keep your cells alive and well functioning as long as possible by following a sensible routine in the areas of nutrition, smoking, and exercise and by knowing the effects of alcohol, drugs and air pollution.

(2) Give your cells extra protection by adding to your diet certain chemical compounds that prevent cell damage and deactivate harmful materials.

(3) To prevent the effects that constitute aging take chemical compounds that slow down or even stop the factors causing aging.

(4) Rejuvenate your cells by replacing damaged materials with perfect and undamaged materials. The "Nucleic Acid Treatment" is one of these methods where the damaged nucleic acids of the cells are replaced by undamaged or new nucleic acids from young cells.

(5) Use surgical methods in order to maintain your youthful appearance, e.g. face lifts, plastic surgery, hair transplants, etc.

(6) In old age your body becomes somewhat inefficient in producing compounds that are necessary for the good functioning of your system.

Three of them are hormones, enzymes and RNA. There are ways to supply your body with these compounds.

Researchers are also at work on reversing aging by removing the effects that constitute aging; a small part of this problem is already solved.

I pointed out earlier that the maximum possible life span for the species man is between 120 and 130 years. Science can also determine the maximum possible life span for animals, and it seems that this maximum life span is difficult to surpass though researchers are working on the problem of extending the limit set by mother nature. But it is definitely possible to reach this limit with a healthier and younger body. In other words: Since you have to die, you want to make sure that you preserve a youthful body for as long as possible.

There are also a few experiments with animals that show that it *will* be possible to extend life expectancy past the maximum.

CHAPTER 4

Energy Is What Your Body Needs

"The greatest hope for increasing life spans can be offered if nutrition—from the time of prenatal development to old age—is continuously of the highest quality."

ROGER J. WILLIAMS
Nutrition Against Disease
p. 144.

The following chapter deals with nutrition and the basic materials which make up the body. I will explain carbohydrates, fats, proteins, vitamins, enzymes, and minerals, and discuss the basic role they play in your body. But keep in mind that this chapter is not a complete guide to good nutrition. The material covered in the following pages will merely give you a general idea about nutrition and will help you to understand material discussed in later chapters.

A good summary on nutrition would take at least 150 pages. However, the topic of nutrition has already been covered by a few writers who combine a good training in the area of biochemistry with a gift for words so as to make this difficult topic easily understood. At the end of this chapter I recommend two books in this field for additional reading. There are other good books in this area, but it is simply too time consuming to read every book on the market.

A longer, happier, healthier and sexier life must start with "super-nutrition." Your first assignment, therefore, will be to do some additional reading in this field. Don't think that you know everything about nutrition until you have read a book by an expert and have seriously examined your eating habits. THIS IS SUPER DUPER IMPORTANT!!!

Why is super-nutrition of such great importance? I would like to give you a quote from "Nutrition Against Disease" by R. Williams: "According to a London study, seventeen delinquent girls (eleven to fifteen years of age) had been on a diet made up largely of white bread and margarine, cheap jam, lots of sweet tea, canned and processed meats. When their diet was changed to one that was far more nutritious and diversified, not only did their complexions and physical well-being improve "almost beyond recognition," but they quickly became less aggressive and quarrelsome. Bad habits seemed to disappear; the "problem children" became less of a problem, and the bored ones began to take an interest in life. There are many results of nutrition studies that demonstrate the importance of good nutrition in respect to appearance, personality and behavior but what we want to do is to take a closer look at how our body processes are affected by nutrition.

Life starts with the production and growth of a large variety of different molecules in the cell, such as fats, proteins, enzymes, DNA, RNA and many others. These molecules account for the most basic functions of the cell. For your cells and organs to function satisfactorily, they need to be supplied with building materials that will maintain an efficient reaction level. This is absolutely necessary. If your body is not supplied with ALL the right nutrients, they can slow down, inhibit or interfere with the most basic functions of your system.

You can actually compare your body to a factory where automobiles are manufactured. In order to make a good automobile, a factory needs all the basic parts; and these parts have to be well engineered and fulfill all specifications. However, if the factory's supply of spark plugs is stopped, it is still possible that there might be a few spare, old or defective plugs to substitute for the new one; but eventually there will be neither spark plugs nor running automobiles.

In some cases with these vehicles, the single parts are not really basic necessities and the car could still be driven without them. For instance, it is possible to construct an automobile without bumpers, signals, seats and shock absorbers. But what would be the efficiency or life span of such a car, and who would want to buy it?

Compare these automobiles to the cells in the body. Nutrients supply basic building materials or the formation of new compounds such as proteins and enzymes; they also supply us with the fuel and lubricants to keep everything running smoothly. If we don't take in certain proteins, then we seriously slow down the maintenance of all parts of the body; and if we don't take in enough vitamins and minerals (the spark plugs and lubricants), then many other body processes are slowed down or completely inhibited. How long will a car engine run on very bad oil? How long will it run without oil?

This definite need for proteins, vitamins, minerals and all the other nutrients is a very good reason why you should not start a crash diet and eat nothing but useless filler materials. If you do not supply your body with a daily minimum of ALL nutrients, you are putting extreme stress on your entire system, and it will accelerate aging tremendously. Further, many missynthesized proteins will be formed because without the proper building materials this is simply what you can expect. The important idea to remember here is that even while dieting your body must still get energy

41

from some source. During crash or starvation diets, the body derives its energy from fat deposits (that's how you take off weight); but the body will also lose some of the structural proteins which give it a nice, firm shape. Besides, the oxidation products that arise from fats can be quite harmful to your body. When you start eating again, the fat is easily redeposited, but not the structural proteins that give the body firmness. In order to maintain a good firm shape you have to exercise and also maintain a sensible diet. To repeat, crash diets without exercising will only accelerate your aging process and change a firm shape into flab. Also, to maintain a well functioning system and a firm shape while dieting, you must supply your body with a minimum of all basic nutrients: food that's high in proteins, vitamins and minerals but low in fats and carbohydrates.

Now let's take a look at some facts. The following are connected with faulty nutrition: anemia, edema, diarrhea, constipation, ulcers, high blood pressure, infections, kidney stones, heart difficulties, senility, impotence, stiffening of the joints, cataracts in the eye, nervous and mental diseases, tuberculosis and many more. It is also a fact that overweight people have a shorter life expectancy and that the memory processes in our brain are strongly dependent upon protein synthesis (91). Hence: bad nutrition, bad protein synthesis, bad memory.

The information that follows will briefly explain what foods contain and why excellent nutrition is important to health. A little knowledge about foods is necessary for understanding the different aging mechanisms. If you want to prolong your life and if you are thinking about taking youth drugs, you must start with good nutrition or, as Professor Williams terms it, "super-nutrition."

WHOM DO YOU ASK IF YOU WANT TO KNOW

MORE ABOUT NUTRITION? Most people think that their doctor is a good source for information on good nutrition. WRONG. Even many doctors agree that the medical profession doesn't know enough about nutrition. The training of our doctors is mainly directed towards healing and curing illnesses. Preventing illnesses by superb nutrition is sadly neglected in almost every medical education program. It is most likely that your doctor went through medical school without ever taking a course in nutrition. If the biochemistry course he took was not up-to-date or if he took the course several years ago and if he is a typical doctor, which means being always busy and never having time to dig into new biochemistry books, then his knowledge about the basic body processes is close to zero. Just take a walk through a hospital and look at the doctors. Are they such healthy specimens? Doctors should know more about nutrition, but we should not expect them to teach us nutrition—they are already overburdened and there are more important things for them to do. I say this because nutrition is actually very simple and should be taught in high school in a general course on health.

In a recent article Professor R. Williams explored the topic of nutrition in depth and stated that the primary cause of noninfective disease is poor nutrition. "Super-nutrition," as he calls it, could prevent many types of disease. His recent book *Nutrition Against Disease* is a masterpiece in this field and should be required reading for everybody, especially for future doctors. Further, the health of our entire nation could be improved dramatically if a course in good nutrition were taught in all high schools and colleges.

There is also a definite relationship between the life span and the amount of food eaten during the course of a day. Dr. C. McCay of Cornell University demonstrated in some experiments that animals live longer when underfed. Rats, when put on a diet which was low in calories, lived approximately 60% longer than the control group. Other researchers confirmed these findings with other kinds of animals. In all these experiments, it was also observed that the animals didn't reach their full size; their growth was somewhat stunted.

What would happen if we restricted the caloric intake for humans? Would we ever reach a height of five feet or more? How long would we live, 150 years? Well, nobody has ever conducted these experiments on humans. But let us draw our conclusions after we have learned a little more about the different aging mechanisms.

Carbohydrates, fats, proteins, vitamins, enzymes and minerals, all play an important role in cell metabolism and the aging process. A little knowledge in this area will help you understand the basic facts about aging.

1. *Proteins:* A protein contains the elements Carbon (C), Hydrogen (H), Oxygen (O), Nitrogen (N) and sometimes Sulphur (S) or other elements. When these elements combine in certain different ratios, they form the basic building blocks of proteins, the amino acids. Our body can synthesize (make) some of these amino acids; those it cannot synthesize in sufficient quantities are called "essential" amino acids and must be supplied. When different amino acids are combined in varying percentages and frequencies, the body produces certain proteins. This is why it is important that if you take protein preparations, you make sure that these preparations contain the essential amino acids, and in the right percentages. The essential amino acids are Arginine (ARG), Histidine (HIS), Isoleucine (ILEU), Lysine (LYS), Methionine (MET), Phenylalanine (PHE), Threonine (TRY) and Valine (VAL).

When you take in protein, it is first hydrolized (broken down) into its amino acids. The amino acids are then transported through the blood stream to your cells where they can be used to make the proteins that characterize the cell's molecular structure (this process will be referred to as "body-characteristic." Significantly, amino acids containing sulfur play an important role in slowing down the aging process; but I will explain this later. Proteins, then, are fundamental to every living material; they provide every cell in the body with its basic composition.

Just recently there were indications that amino acids might also be the universal building blocks of life. Eighteen different amino acids and two pyrimidines (DNA bases) were found on meteorites by Dr. C. Ponnamperuma and co-workers at NASA's Ames Research Center (7). At a meeting of the New York Academy of Sciences, Dr. Ponnamperuma disclosed that six of these 18 amino acids are found in living cells on earth; the other 12 and the two DNA bases were only similar to chemicals found on earth.

Your body can obtain the needed proteins that contain all the required amino acids from milk, milk products, eggs, meat, fish, liver, poultry, brewer's yeast and many sources. The best way to assure the right supply of the correct proteins is to eat more than one type of protein at a time. If one kind is lacking a certain amino acid, the other will probably have it. The average recommended amounts of proteins are 70 grams for an adult man and 60 grams for an adult woman (per day). Since you want to make sure that you always get enough proteins, you should try to eat at least 20 grams more per day than recommended. If you ever eat too much protein, your body can store a small quantity and will convert other excess proteins into sugar; but that happens very seldom. If your body lacks proteins, it will take apart the least important body proteins in order to get the amino acids required for more important processes. But if we are talking about keeping our system in top shape, is there any protein that can be called less important?

There are thousands of different proteins in our body, and each one requires the right amounts of essential amino acids. A decrease in the efficiency of your organs in old age is directly related to a decreased and faulty protein synthesis in your body. It is therefore of the utmost importance to supply the body at all times with good proteins.

The following lists what will happen to you if your diet does not contain all essential amino acids:

a) The maintenance of all organs and body proteins will be hampered.

b) The thinking and memory processes will weaken.

c) Several hormones will not be formed since they depend upon proteins for satisfactory synthesis.

d) The correct enzymes cannot be formed because enzymes are basicly proteins.

e) The formation of antibodies and other defenses which protect us from bacteria and other toxic materials will be seriously hampered because they are made of proteins.

Making a protein is just impossible for your body if the necessary amino acids are not available. It's like asking a manufacturer to make machine parts made of iron only; if the man doesn't have any iron, he just can't do it no matter what you promise him or how hard you push him.

2. *Carbohydrates*: Carbohydrates in their most basic forms are called "simple sugars." In plants, with the help of chlorophyll and light energy, these simple sugars are made from carbon dioxide and water. Glucose and deoxyribose are the most important sugars, and deoxyribose is the sugar in the structure of DNA.

Chains of different sugars make up other carbohydrates such as starch.

Glucose is the sugar in your blood that can be converted to "instant energy." More complicated sugars have to be broken down into simple sugars and glucose first before they can be oxidized to give energy. And since the glucose level in your blood is your basic energy source, you must keep it at a suitable level at all times. The way NOT to do this is to eat large quantities of sweets. If you do this, you are actually asking your body to convert the sugar into fat, which is the last thing you want to happen. You can maintain a healthy sugar level in your blood simply by eating foods high in proteins.

3. *Lipids*: The simplest lipids are called fats. The basic building blocks of lipids are glycerol and fatty acids (1 glycerol + 3 fatty acids = 1 fat). More complicated lipids contain other elements like phosphorus, e.g. phospholipids. The fats in foods are hydrolized in your system into the simple components and then transported to the cells, where they can be oxidized to give energy or reassembled into body characteristic fats and stored as such. Remember, though, that small quantities of fats are needed in your system because they serve to protect nerve ends and are also good insulators against low temperatures.

There are also other essential fatty acids that your body cannot make itself and that must be supplied from your diet. Linoleic acid and linolenic are two that are lacking in most diets due to processing of foods. You can easily balance this deficiency by taking daily two or three teaspoons of safflower oil, which contains a high percentage of linoleic acid. Why these essential fatty acids are so important is explained in a question in Chapter 20.

4. *Vitamins and Minerals* cannot be synthesized by your body; therefore you must supply your body

with adequate amounts of these compounds. The importance of vitamins is generally known. But a few vitamins, such as vitamins E, C and B, deserve special attention and will be discussed in more detail in the chapters that deal with slowing down aging mechanisms and preventing arteriosclerosis.

Until a few years ago it was believed that only very small quantities of vitamins were necessary for a well-functioning body. You probably learned in high school that deficiencies of certain vitamins are the cause of some diseases: for instance, you were probably told that vitamin D deficiency inhibits blood clotting and leads to prolonged bleeding after an injury, and that vitamin K is necessary for biochemical reactions involving phosphorus.

Vitamin A deficiency causes the hardening of several kinds of tissue in our body and is called keratinization. For example, keratinization of the eye is a hardening of the tear ducts that causes a decreased secretion of tears and results in inefficient eye washing and lubrication.

Vitamin B_1, B_2 and B_{12} deficiency leads to deceased appetite, loss of weight, or beriberi. Other results from vitamin B deficiencies include inflammation of certain body tissues, incomplete carbohydrate metabolism, and decreased capacity of the body to produce certain amino acids.

Niacin deficiency leads to an illness called pellegra, rough skin and inflammation of the mouth.

Pyroxidine deficiencies lead to irritable behavior and a decreased amino acid metabolism.

A biotin deficiency can cause symptoms ranging from muscle pain to depression.

These are just a few examples of what can happen if the body lacks certain vitamins. There are hundreds of other effects that a lack of vitamins can cause, but they're too complicated to describe here.

During the last few years scientists have been taking a new look at the effects of large doses of vitamins in the body. IS IT TRUE WHAT MANY DOCTORS SAY ABOUT VITAMINS? "A well-balanced diet contains all the vitamins your body needs; vitamins are needed only in extremely small quantities." DEFINITELY NOT. Here are some research results:

W. Kaufman studied diseases of the joints and found that large quantities of a B vitamin remarkably relieved stiffening in a very short time (9).

I. Stone, a biochemist, has studied vitamin C extensively and believes that vitamin C is absolutely necessary for maintaining good health. Stone studied some animals that can produce vitamin C in their system. He then compared the weight and vitamin C formation in test animals in proportion to an average human body weight and determined that a rat would produce as much as 15 grams of vitamin C when under stress if it weighed as much as a human (10).

Linus Pauling suggests large doses of vitamin C as a cure for the common cold. He was scolded by the medical profession for stepping onto their "holy ground." But whatever the medical opinion about vitamin C is, I can vouch that it has worked for me. I used to get such bad colds that I literally had to hide for a week from friends and neighbors. Now when I feel a cold coming on I take up to eight grams (8,000 milligrams) of vitamin C per day. I haven't had a really bad cold in years.

Professor R. Mumma's findings with test animals show that vitamin C increased cholesterol excretion in test animals (11). But I will analyze the cholesterol problem in Chapter 13. Also Dr. F. Klenner has treated simple infectious diseases, polio, measles and mumps, with a sodium salt of vitamin C and has reported positive results (12).

Professor R. Williams has reported that whenever

the absorption of vitamin A was very slow, an excess of vitamin E stimulated the vitamin A uptake (13). As we will see in Chapters 5 and 20, vitamin E is also being tested with other compounds as an age retarding drug.

The research team of L. Buch, R. Halpern, R. Smith, D. Streeter, L. Simon and M. Stout reported in *Biochemistry Journal* that a B vitamin can inhibit a tumor enzyme (14).

W. Bollag and F. Ott have also used a vitamin A acid to treat skin tumors. Out of their 60 patients, 27 responded partially and 24 effectively (15)—the remaining showed no effect from the treatment.

Stomach ulcers can also be controlled by vitamin A. When ulcers form in the lining of the stomach, new cells cannot be formed at a proper rate. As a result protective materials are not excreted, and the ulcers eat right through the stomach walls. Vitamin A speeds up the formation of healthy cells and prevents the formation of ulcers. That vitamin A can prevent the formation of ulcers was confirmed by tests performed on both animals and humans.

Vitamin D, which is often classified as a hormone, controls bone formation by releasing calcium into the blood stream. The fact that hyperparathyroid women have difficulties in delivering healthy babies is due to thyroid problems that interfere with the bone formation of the fetus. Vitamin D research has recently helped several women have healthy babies.

Vitamin E protects the walls of cells. Anemic children treated at Case Western Reserve University with large doses of vitamin E showed excellent improvements.

High doses of several different vitamins, up to several hundred times the normal amounts, were also used by many psychiatrists to treat mental illness like schizophrenia, also with excellent results.

5. *Enzymes*: Enzymes can be synthesized by the body and are needed only in extremely small quantities. Almost every reaction in our metabolism is controlled by an enzyme which serves a specific function. For example, the enzyme protease is concerned only with the hydrolysis of proteins and the enzymes lipase and carbohydrase are solely responsible for the hydrolysis of lipids and carbohydrates. So you see, every metabolic reaction needs a specific enzyme.

The formation of enzymes is controlled by DNA. Since enzymes are mainly proteins composed of different amino acids in varying percentages and frequencies, the two most important factors for good enzyme formation in our cells are (1) an undamaged DNA and (2) the supply of the correct nutrients. If your cells do not have the basic building materials for the enzymes, then the enzymes cannot be produced.

For example, a damaged DNA molecule will give wrong instructions for enzyme synthesis and will create enzymes that cannot perform their functions.

In older age, the chance that missynthesized enzymes will be formed by the damaged DNA is increased tremendously. If you were able to substitute inefficient enzymes for good, well functioning ones, you could really "tune up" your metabolism (all biochemical reactions). Some people do this already by taking commercially available enzymes. The shelves of health food stores are stocked with many enzyme preparations.

H. and D. Gershon have detected inactive enzyme molecules in aging organisms. There is evidence that inactive (missynthesized?) enzymes actually exist and don't do the job they are designed for (16). Other researchers have also demonstrated that there is a definite difference between the enzymes formed in old and young animals (120).

Even though it might be a good idea to substitute
51

good enzymes for bad ones in older age, I don't believe that you should stuff yourself with commercially produced enzymes when the young body can still handle the situation efficiently. If the body takes in certain enzymes constantly, it might stop making them itself and therefore might not be able to restart this synthesis at a required time. From what we know about the mechanisms of these enzyme reactions there is no real danger that this could happen, but why take a chance?

Nutrition experts continue to argue about the importance of supplying the body with enzymes. Enzymes are found in many foods, but since they are proteins, they can be destroyed by the cooking process. Fresh and uncooked foods can, therefore, increase the enzyme supply to your body. Besides, enzyme synthesis uses up energy, and if we supply these enzymes to the body, its energy resources can be used for any number of energy requiring processes.

The above are important problems that we must seriously consider, and research results help clarify them.

6. *Hormones* are chemical messengers which are made by the hormone glands in very small quantities. They control enzyme reactions and keep our system and organs ticking at the right speed. The endocrine glands that synthesize the hormones in our body are the pituitary, thyroid, parathyroid, adrenal, pancreas, intestine and the gonads. The hormones are excreted by the glands directly into the blood stream and are very specific in their points of action. Many of the hormones are proteins or have a protein part. Super nutrition will supply the building blocks for the synthesis of these hormones.

In old age hormones decrease in concentration. Sometimes it is possible to make up the difference by taking hormones but as soon as you stop taking them you are back to where you started. In one experiment with old animals we are trying to revitalize the endocrine glands in order to keep the entire body functioning better in old age. The experiment is still going on but about 30 per cent of the animals in the control group have already died.

It will be quite a while until we know more about hormones and longevity. Some results by other researchers are discussed in chapter 15 and a little more about hormone treatments you will find in chapter 9.

A healthy life style and good exercise will keep your endocrine system functioning for the longest time possible.

7. *Minerals*: Minerals are another group of compounds needed by the body. These compounds have to be supplied in your diet since your body has no other way to produce them. The following summary shows the distribution of minerals in the body.

Phosphorus is needed for bone formation and for maintaining a constant acid-base level in body fluids. Phosphorus is also involved in several other energy transfer reactions in other metabolic processes.

Calcium is found in bones and in blood plasma. Vitamin D accelerates the absorption of calcium, and the amount of calcium in the blood is necessary to stabilize many cell functions.

Magnesium is found mainly in bones but also in muscles. It is also an important agent for certain enzyme reactions.

Sodium, potassium and chlorine are needed to maintain a constant salt concentration in the blood and other fluids; the sodium/potassium balance plays an important role in nerve reactions. Iodine is required to regulate the function of the thyroid gland which in turn produces several different hormones. Simple goiter is due to an iodine deficiency.

The action of fluorine is difficult to study, but it is

believed that a small quantity is necessary for good, healthy teeth.

Iron is the central atom in the blood molecule. A woman needs more iron due to the loss of blood in the menstrual cycle. Too much iron is not good for your body. If you are taking iron and vitamin E, don't take these two at the same time.

Zinc is necessary for the formation of an enzyme called carbonic anhydrase.

Manganese is stored in the liver and kidney and is believed to be involved in many enzyme reactions.

The copper needs of our systems are not well defined, but it appears that copper can prevent anemia.

Molybdenum is needed for certain enzymes and researchers think that it might work with copper in the formation of blood cells.

Cobalt is found in a B vitamin.

Selenium is quite toxic in its salt form, but it might be needed as part of an amino acid. Amino acids that contain selenium are being tested by R. Passwater as drugs that might slow down the aging process (17).

I had planned to work out a table of minimum requirements of nutrients, vitamins and minerals; but Professor R. Williams has suggested not to do this since daily nutrient requirements vary quite a bit from person to person due to differences in weight, activity and biochemical individuality.

Since many good books have been written on the topic of nutrition, it is mainly important to know what foods contain and what role they play in the aging process. Only the basic and most important facts have been discussed here and it would be worthwhile for you to do some additional reading about nutrition. Of the many books about nutrition, I would recommend *Nutrition against Disease* by Professor R. Williams. Professor Williams is a leading nutrition expert, the discoverer of a B vitamin, and director of the Clayton

Foundation Biochemical Institute at the University of Texas. He was also one of the many scientists who have recently raised serious doubts about the nutritional value of many of our ordinary foods.

In order to understand what foods are and what they contain, you will need a table of foods and their contents. It is important to know how many calories these foods contain, but it is even more important to know WHAT these foods contain. Counting calories only is not enough. The books by A. Davis contain good tables of foods and their contents and are available in less expensive paperbacks. You should be familiar with the contents of the major foods you eat.

ON DIETS: The Medical Diet Drama unfolded itself in front of our eyes when a major TV network had three weight-control MD's discussing diets and how to lose weight. They hardly agreed on anything and I wouldn't wonder if the entirely confused viewer said "to hell with it" and kept on eating. But let me discuss some of the highlights of this discussion and air my views:

MD no. 1: Dr. Stillman. The major diet discussed was his protein, lots of water and one vitamin pill diet. Nutritionally this is about the worst type of diet that was discussed on the show. The diet works alright, but only because it messes up your body so badly that it has no chance but to lose weight. But this is not the only thing you might lose. From the viewpoint of long-term health and the damage this diet might do to your system, I have only one word of advice: DON'T. I am presently collecting data to show that one ages about 10 to 15 times the normal rate while on such a diet. MD no. 2: Dr. N. Solomon. Author of *The Truth About Weight Control,* he attacked the problem from a very scientific standpoint, and at first I was impressed and bought his book. Here are a few things I just couldn't agree with. The importance of a good cross section of different proteins is not efficiently emphasized in the book (nor was it in the TV discussion). Rule no. 4 in Chapter 2 is "Eat half-portions of whatever you would normally eat." I don't really think Dr. Solomon would have stated that rule if he knew what kind of junk some people eat. It seems he also has not recognized the dangers of too many carbohydrates. In a test diet he also recommends coffee or tea with every meal when it should be well known in the medical world that too much coffee can be quite harmful. The major thing I objected to was his constant advice to consult a doctor. It is a well established fact that doctors don't know too much about nutrition and dieting, so why waste your money? I believe that the majority of people can lose weight by following some sensible rules. If it is still impossible for a person to achieve and maintain a normal weight, then one of the weight control centers recommended by Dr. Solomon should be visited and some money spent on important tests. Malfunctions in your body can be the cause of your obesity and a "good" diet will not correct these malfunctions. If you are concerned about your long-term health and aging, you must learn how to prevent what Dr. Solomon terms the "Yo Yo Syndrome"; the constant gain and loss of weight can cause serious malfunctions in your body. Dr. Solomon also seems to be set against taking more than the RDA amounts of vitamins, which is in line with the AMA and FDA, but as you will see in other chapters in this book, I have serious doubts about many decisions of the AMA and FDA. If you have a serious weight problem or want to prevent one, read Dr. Solomons' book—but with reservations. MD no. 3: Dr. Atkins, a diet doctor with a good record—so he claims. What is his diet? Proteins and a good amount of fat foods and extra vitamins. Dr. Atkins has obviously recognized the importance of adding enough vitamins to a diet but he completely eliminates carbohydrates from it. Even though an excess of carbohydrates can be quite harmful, we should not eliminate them completely from our diet. We also know that a major cause for atherosclerosis is the presence of triglycerides (fats) in the blood which is almost directly proportional to the amounts of fat foods eaten. I am well aware of the fact that many of the high-fat diets that prompted these conclusions also contained high quantities of carbohydrates and that other studies suggest that carbohydrates are even more dangerous than fats in respect to atherosclerosis. But eliminating carbohydrates and increasing fats in a diet is a bit too risky for my taste. I am also concerned about your long-term health, while a diet doctor's primary concern is to get the fat off. My own diet recommendations are not exactly what an average doctor would call a "balanced diet," though I also recommend a reduced carbohydrate and an increased protein intake. However, if it is not possible for you to lose weight by following some sensible rules, Dr. Atkins' diet is probably the best. His book is titled *Dr. Atkins' Diet Revolution.*

One thing all three MD's were able to agree on: Exercise is very important both to lose weight and to maintain a normal weight.

Another message came across quite clearly: If you want to lose weight, DON'T use diet pills.

And now I would like to give you my rules about nutrition.

SOME GOOD RULES ABOUT NUTRITION AND HOW TO LOSE WEIGHT WITHOUT DOING ANY HARM TO YOUR SYSTEM:

You have seen that the body needs a variety of different foodstuffs in order to function properly; therefore you want to make sure that your body gets all the nutrients it needs. If you want to lose weight, you just cut down on food quantities and eat reasonably. You must eat a cross section of ALL foods even when you lose weight; this is important for your long-term health. When it comes to eating, you sometimes just have to practice a little self-discipline.

When it comes to food quantities, we just don't know how much food man requires. For persons of the same weight and sex, the food intake can vary as much as two-fold, so that one person lives normally on a certain amount of food, while the other gets fat. Food requirements and energy expenditure depend very much on *your* metabolism. Four British experts published a paper on this topic (151).

1) Chew all your food well and only keep putting more food in your mouth when you are really hungry. Cut down on the salt you take in. Take one to two teaspoons of safflower oil or any other oil that contains high quantities of essential fatty acids once a day after a meal.

2) Eat foods high in proteins and very low in carbohydrates and fats. Start each day with a high protein breakfast, containing at least two to three different proteins. Good proteins are milk and milk products, eggs, fish, poultry, lean meat, brewer's yeast and many others. Familiarize yourself with the table of food contents in respect to carbohydrates, fats, proteins and vitamins. This is much more important than just limiting your caloric intake. You will find many other foods that are high in proteins. If you eat right you don't have to worry about the cholesterol in eggs. Eat only very small quantities of potatoes, bread or fat foods. Forget about noodles, pastries, cookies, sweets, sugar, rolls, butter, cream, rich salad dressings and any kind of sweet soda.

3) Drink at least one glass of multi-vegetable juice per day. Eat some fruits, but not too many, because fruits are often high in carbohydrates. Also eat some fresh, uncooked vegetables and salads. Don't boil your foods because the cooking process destroys many valuable compounds. Whenever you have a choice between fresh or canned fruits and vegetables, choose the fresh. Canned foods contain preservatives which are not toxic in small quantities, but why take a chance? Don't drink any artificial breakfast drinks. Vitamins are still being discovered, but if you drink orange juice, grapefruit or vegetable juices you still have the best chance of getting what your body needs, and these juices also contain minerals. A juicer (different from a mixer, approximately $50 in a major department store) extracts the goodness from fresh vegetables and fruits, leaving all the bulky filler materials and some carbohydrates behind. It's a lot of fun to make your own juices with this machine, and it seems that it helps many people to control excess weight by supplying all the catalysts that are needed to burn up excess weight.

4) Always take a good multi-vitamin with minerals and some extra vitamins C, E, A and niacin. Take these vitamins after meals and don't take them at the same time but at different times of the day. Vitamins do not contain calories and you can think of them as the spark plugs in your body. Think of an automobile: first you put in some good fuel, and then you get it running with a good, clean set of spark plugs. Even the best ignition system couldn't get a car running without fuel and with weak plugs.

5) Don't stuff yourself before you go to bed. It will make you fat (or a bad performer, if you think about other activities). Drink a glass of water with

every meal and before you go to sleep. By doing this, you help your body flush out materials that it doesn't need. But don't drink too much water; it might offset the salt balance in your body fluids and that is NOT good.

6) You should always do some exercise; but this is especially important if you want to lose weight. Any physical activity is good even if it only means turning on the radio and dancing to the music at an accelerated speed. Lovemaking is a good exercise too; and if you think that you use only a few calories when making love, you better think about what you are doing wrong in bed.

7) Listen to your body. There are certain appetite regulating mechanisms which actually signal and bring about an appetite for foods that the body needs. Even though this area of research is not thoroughly understood, the experts agree on the existence of such mechanisms.

8) And for God's sake read the label when you buy foods. Does it sound like the inventory of a chemical company?

Don't attempt to lose too much weight at once. Start with reasonable food quantities as outlined above. It is impossible to say exactly how much a person should eat because weight, stress and activity vary so drastically from person to person. If you are not happy with the amount of weight you lose, just reduce the quantities you take, but be sure to get all the nutrients outlined above.

A few more rules about good eating in general. Don't overeat. The mortality ratio is about 50% higher if you are 25% overweight and is about 80% higher if you are 35% overweight.

Watch what your children eat. "Overfed and undernourished" is true for the highest percentage of our children and teenagers. Don't reward them with cookies or other sweets; they'll believe that such foods are good for them.

The bread you eat should have some nutritional value; therefore eat wheat germ or protein bread.

And for the sake of your body DON'T go on diets that prescribe proteins and water only. Many diets that deprive your body of important nutrients, such as the carbohydrate and grapefruit juice diets, will make you lose weight, but they will also seriously damage your body and your health.

If you just want to maintain your present weight, you should eat approximately the same foods and quantities in the light of the above outline.

I was extremely shocked to read in the *Prevention* magazine of September 1972 that the Food and Drug Administration recently staged a raid on a health food store and confiscated vitamin E, cholin and multi-vitamin tablets merely because they were labeled "dietary supplement." The FDA also tries to prevent the packaging of any "nonessential" compounds in capsule form because, they argue, somebody might believe them to be medicine. But this is not all. The FDA also wants to severely restrict what you can buy in vitamins. For example, if a vitamin contains more than 150% of the Recommended Daily Allowance (RDA), then they want it to be labeled as a drug and sold as a drug. That means that 250 mg tablets of vitamin C will be labeled as drugs. The RDA's replace the Minimum Daily Requirements (MDR's) and are approximately twice as much as the MDR's. Naturally vitamin E preparations would also be labeled drugs in the sizes in which we are used to buying them. Do you want to consult a doctor every time you want to get yourself YOUR size of vitamin E, C or A? We all know how expensive drugs and doctor visits are.

The Food and Drug Administration is a branch of

the government which is supposed to watch out for our health. This is an extremely large field which ranges from determining which household paints are safe to use, which foods contain too much of a contaminant and which drugs are safe to use. The agency has been criticized recently for its decisions by leading scientists in the nutrition and health field. Some of the rulings of the FDA are good and absolutely needed, but some of the criticisms make sense.

Some people feel that the regulations and rules of the FDA are too strict and should be changed. Remember the birth defects caused by mothers taking thalidomide? Well, the strict rules of the FDA prevented these accidents here in the US.

Some people want the FDA to rule that preservatives like BHT and BHA should not be allowed in foods. According to a recent study, it seems that these antioxidants are responsible for a decrease of gastric cancer in this country (125). They are also under investigation for use as antiaging drugs (148). All this sounds very good and makes sense, but if you take a closer look at some of the rulings, you just can't rid yourself of the feeling that big business has a strong effect on some of the FDA's rulings and also that some rulings are strongly influenced by a small number of opinionated doctors who are not up-to-date on the latest research results.

If buying 200 mg vitamin E preparations without a prescription is against the law, then buying aspirin containing preparations should be punished by imprisonment and smoking should be a federal offense. And what tops it all is that these proposed regulations are based on hearings on vitamins held by the FDA in 1968-1970 which are already outdated.

Professor Roger Williams and Professor Linus Pauling have clearly demonstrated that the requirements for people of the same weight and height can be very different, so that one person might need up to 100 times as much of a certain vitamin as another person. I believe that certain vitamins play an important role in the aging process, and it should be up to you to decide what and how much you want to take. Think it over and let your government representatives know how you feel about this issue. You can also help the passage of the congressional bill No. HR 2323, which prohibits the government from limiting the potency of any food supplement which is not intrinsically harmful to your health. It is your right to express your opinion to government representatives, or in this case to the Hon. P. Rogers, Chairman, Subcommittee on Public Health, Interstate and Foreign Commerce Committee, Room 2125, Rayburn House Office Building, Washington, D.C., 20515.

PART II

The Newest Discoveries On Aging

Up to just a few years ago there were many different theories on aging—theories with little or no proof at all. Very recently four theories received strong support from new research results. Actually these theories are very closely related and we can call the combination of them "The Combination Theory of Aging." The four theories that have solved a small part of the aging problem are:

1) The DNA Damage Theory
2) The Cross-Link Theory
3) The Free Radical Theory
4) The Stress Theory

Counteracting only ten percent of all the aging factors could lead to a life span of about 170 years.

FOOD

is digested; and car-
bohydrates, fats, and
proteins are con-
verted into

↓

SUGARS—FATTY ACIDS—
GLYCEROL AND AMINO ACIDS ETC.

oxidation of these
compounds provide

these materials can
be used to maintain
your body's efficiency
and to make body
characteristic materials

↓   ↓

ENERGY AND VARIOUS   BODY CHARACTERISTIC
OXIDATION PRODUCTS   SUBSTANCES

some oxidation prod-
ucts are not very sta-
ble and can form very
reactive molecules or
fractions of mole-
cules under the influ-
ence of RADIATION,
FAULTY NUTRITION
(caffeine, sodium ni-
trite etc.), and AIR
POLLUTION: These
very reactive mole-
cules are called

↓

FREE RADICALS

free radicals can
damage almost everything

↓

DNA, RNA, CELL WALLS,
ENZYMES, PROTEINS,
LYSOMES ETC.

CHAPTER 5

Deadly Enemies

"Ozone is another source of radicals. It's frequently overlooked that the normal ozone content of air at sea level, 0.002 PPM, is an extremely significant amount in terms of ability to do damage to living organisms. For comparison, the alert level of ozone in smog in the Los Angeles area is 0.5 PPM. Levels of 10 to 15 PPM ozone kill small mammals in several hours."

WILLIAM A. PRIOR
Chemical and Engineering News
June 7, 1971

In Chapter 2 aging was defined as a constant damage of cells which leads to decreased efficiency and death of the cells. Depending on the type of cells and their chemical make-up, cell damage occurs at different rates. But the most serious damage to the cell occurs when the DNA, the central director of all cell functions, is damaged by agents called "Free Radicals." Free radicals are very reactive molecules or fractions of molecules that are formed mainly from oxidation products of foods. The chemists' definition is that these free radicals carry a single electron. Since all other molecules have electrons in pairs, each time a free radical reacts with a molecule, it forms another radical. It is not really important that you know what a radical is; just remember that it can do a lot of damage.

adical Theory on Aging" was proposed
n who studied the effects of free radical
the life span of LAF$_1$ mice (5). Later
. Eyring, an outstanding chemist at Utah
, revealed that caffeine, sodium nitrite (a
ditive), radiation (from many different
sources) and certain by-products of your metabolism
are the major causes of radical formation and can cause
chromosome damage (18).

Other areas where free radicals can do some serious
damage are the walls of the cells and the organelles
in the cells. Heavy damage here would lead immediately to the death of the entire cell.

Many other revealing studies on the effects of radicals have confirmed these findings.

W. A. Pryor of the Louisiana State University discusses several radical producing mechanisms and the
possible ways of slowing down the aging process by
counteracting these radicals (19). Two articles by R.
A. Passwater and P. A. Welker define what aging is,
and they discuss their own approach to solving the
aging problem. They also believe that free radicals
are a major cause of aging and have introduced a
concept called "Protein Missynthesis Resorters" (discussed in Chapter 6) into the aging theory.

The chemist has a new tool called ESR. This is a
machine that can detect free radicals even in living
tissue. With such a machine the Lenin Prize winner
Nicolai Markovitch Emanuel found that there were
upsurges of free radicals in animals well before the
signs of malignancy were detected by conventional
methods (148,152). This is very interesting, but the
problem with biochemistry is that there is always
another interpretation. For example, in this case the
ESR signal could have been due to the iron complex
which is also present in tumors.

It is not yet entirely clear whether free radicals are

always involved in normal biochemical reactions. However, it is well established that many compounds are formed in your metabolic processes which can easily form radicals under the influence of radiation or certain chemicals in food.

Let's now see what happens to your cells when free radicals are formed:

A radical is formed somewhere in the cell. This radical can now damage the cell material or DNA. If DNA, the central director of your cells, is damaged and not repaired immediately, it will not perform its duties as efficiently as before. The DNA damage can also be carried over to the next cell. Repeated radical damage can therefore lead to the point where the cell completely loses its efficiency. (See Figure 8 for a schematic representation.) An increase in missynthesized materials, caused by the damaged DNA, interferes with the cell functions and can also cause adverse immunological reactions, which again puts more stress on your system and speeds up the aging process. What can you do about this? First, do not take in compounds in your foods that can cause radical formations. Since scientists are discovering more information about this problem, I believe that within two or three years a list of the foods, food preservatives and other compounds that you should avoid will be available. What can you do in the meantime? What would you normally do when you have a problem? First you study its characteristics. It is like finding the cure for an illness. If its cause is a bacteria, which antibiotic inhibits its growth? Can the body, affected by this bacteria, tolerate the antibiotic without experiencing side effects? This area has been investigated by numerous researchers. A big advantage for us. Once we know the path of a chemical reaction (the mechanism), we can try to interfere with it, accelerate it, slow it down or even stop it.

Figure 9.

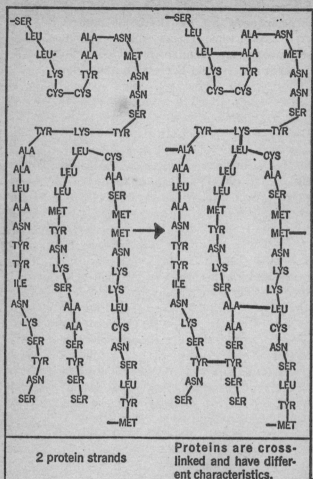

| 2 protein strands | Proteins are cross-linked and have different characteristics. |

Since scientists possess much knowledge about the chemistry of radicals, they can create a large number of compounds that can deactivate radicals. To our great surprise some of these radical deactivators, called antioxidants, are found in many foods. Sulfur amino acids and vitamin E are such antioxidants.

Now let's study this theory. If it is true that sulfur amino acids and vitamin E can deactivate radicals in your body, then cell damaging effects could be decreased and your life span increased. Tests with animals have already shown that their life span, depending on the antioxidant used, can be extended from eight to 30% (20). When several different antioxidants were used in combination, a 167% extension of the average life expectancy of mice was achieved (1). However, to measure positive effects on humans is not so easy. The difficulty arises from constructing valid tests. A scientist simply cannot feed these drugs (or better, youth compounds) to hundreds of people and then wait for them to die in order to check the increase in their life span. But more about this in Chapter 14.

Yet these antioxidants are not widely used. It always takes the medical profession quite a while to "make sure." These research results are also of a very recent nature and some of them taste and smell pretty bad. But the latter is not a real problem since many bad tasting drugs taken internally are merely put in a gelatin capsule and swallowed without bad taste. The capsule dissolves in the stomach and the compounds can go to work.

Up to this point I have only discussed the radicals' damaging effect on DNA; but damage caused by radicals is far more devastating. I pointed out earlier that there are many different theories on aging. One theory suggests that aging is a constant cross-linking of molecules to each other; proteins, nucleic acids, almost everything can be cross-linked. (21). This is basically an alteration of your body chemicals which can also be explained by the radical theory. It is an easy task for a chemist to show that proteins for example, when exposed to free radicals, form cross-links. Let me explain this: (See Figure 6.)

Proteins are basically long chains of amino acids that are linked together. When cross-linking occurs they are no longer body characteristic proteins because their structure has been altered. Radical interceptors (antioxidants) should prevent at least part of these cross-links. Cross-linking is discussed in more detail in the next chapter.

STOP! Before you run out to get yourself a large supply of vitamin E and other antioxidants, I would suggest that you ask your doctor if he knows any reason why YOU should not take these compounds. For instance you might be allergic or you might have an ailment that prevents you from taking these chemicals. Don't ask him what he thinks about your wanting to take these compounds. You might get an outdated opinion on the subject. It is a sad fact that many doctors don't know too much biochemistry and are also so very busy that they don't have the time to keep up with the latest research.

CHAPTER 6

Your Body Can Make Mistakes

*"Cross-linking agents can be visualized as lit-
tle rods with two hooks which link together
two giant molecules. There are probably hundreds of ways to describe the cross-linkage
effect, the way two things are tied together
so as to impede the motion of the other. Sup-
pose someone went around handcuffing together thousands of workers in a large factory.
Efficiency, naturally, would drop. The entire
operation would be paralyzed unless means
were found to remove the handcuffs faster
than they were being put on."*

Dr. Johan Bjorksten

Imagine that you are standing at the construction
site of a new high-rise building. On the top of the
building are several large cranes moving construction
material up and down. Now some saboteur comes
along and ties two of the cranes' long steel ropes together. This will definitely slow down or even completely stop the work of two cranes; and if more ropes
are cross-linked with each other, the entire construction of the building will come to a stop.

In our living systems we have a similar chemical
process that prevents optimum cell efficiency (21).
Protein molecules are long chains of amino acids linked
together. These long protein molecules are very
often parallel and close together. Often cross-linking
agents form bonds between these molecules, tying
them together in a covalent bond formation. Covalent

73

bonds are very strong and, once formed, are very difficult to remove. As a result, the properties of the protein molecules are now drastically changed and are not body characteristic any more.

Professor Standinger demonstrated how the physical characteristics of large molecules are drastically changed by cross-linking. He showed that only one cross-linkage for every 30,000 units of a large molecule is enough to change its solubility and many other physical characteristics (22). The cross-linked proteins then interfere with the normal cell functions, performing their own duties less efficiently. The biggest problem, however, is when cross-linking continues and the large molecules formed in this process are not removed. An increase of cross-linking occurs naturally with age. This has been demonstrated and discussed by many researchers (23, 24, 25). In a specific case age pigments (or lipofuscins) are such polymeric molecules (26).

As discussed by Bjorksten (21), several groups of compounds, called "cross-linking agents," can cause bonds between molecules. Some of these cross-linking agents are oxidation products of our metabolism, free radicals and heavy metals like lead. Bjorksten originally estimated that free radicals do about five to ten percent of the cross-linking. However, in the light of recent radical research in living tissue, this number is probably much higher. But this is not the whole picture. Since cross-linked molecules are much bigger than the original molecules, they are not recognized by the body as body characteristic. Thus, immunologic reactions against (rejections of) these molecules begin and the body literally attacks itself.

The collagen theory on aging deals with the cross-linking of collagen, a supporting protein which makes up approximately 40% of our total protein. The shrinking of these cross-links strangles many healthy cells.

There are also some good indications that enzymes might be involved in the bond formation of collagen (27). The question arises as to whether this is a controlled, planned aging process. Well, whatever it is, there are ways to deactivate or slow down the action of specific enzymes, and there is no problem if these bonds are "undone" faster than they are made.

When DNA molecules divide they are also close and parallel; cross-linking at this time can completely destroy parts of the information on DNA.

It is of great interest to note that researchers are working on both sides of the problem. One group is trying to prevent cross-links from being formed (Passwater et al.). The other group is trying to find ways to undo these damaging bonds (Bjorksten and others), once they have been formed. Both groups are making progress and it is only a question of time and money before they find the answer. It would be fantastic if both of them came up with an answer. We could then prevent bond formation and stop aging, and we could also destroy existing bonds and totally reverse the aging process.

There is one more major way in which proteins can be formed that is not body characteristic, namely by a DNA initiated synthesis. We have seen earlier that the synthesis of proteins is controlled by the central director, the DNA. Let's review quickly how this happens: If the formation of a protein is necessary somewhere in the cell, first a messenger RNA is formed on the DNA (like a blueprint of the original instructions). This messenger RNA travels to the site where the protein is required and there, with the help of the transfer RNA, the synthesis takes place. If the instructions were copies from a damaged DNA, then the messenger RNA also carries some incomplete or incorrect instructions which again lead to a missynthesized protein which is not body characteristic.

Once a missynthesized protein is formed from the amino acids, the body doesn't really know what to do with it and this protein is not incorporated into our body proteins immediately—it just sits around for a while. This is lucky for us, because while these missynthesized proteins wait to be incorporated into our body protein, we can expose them to chemicals that might actually take apart the missynthesized proteins, preventing the incorporation of these mistakes into the body structure. This also means that the amino acids will be returned to the "materials pool" where they can be used again to make the correct proteins. Absolute proof has not yet been published, but a large amount of supporting data and facts have been collected by R. Passwater (28). Sulfur amino acids which are radical deactivators are also being tested as "protein missynthesis resorters" by Dr. Passwater.

Sulfur amino acids are cystein, cystine and methionine. The importance of sulfur amino acids is well recognized by many researchers and has already led to some confusion about nutrition. One nutrition group suggests we eat more eggs because they contain high concentrations of sulfur amino acids. Another group tells us not to eat eggs because they contain too much cholesterol. So what should we do? Professor Mumma found that vitamin C increases the cholesterol excretion in test animals. If this holds true for humans we are in business. All we would have to do is to eat lots of eggs together with some vitamin C and everybody should be happy! Linus Pauling feels that vitamin C is helpful for curing a common cold and that its toxicity is extremely low. The work of the biochemist I. Stone, who prompted Linus Pauling to write his book on vitamin C, suggests an answer to us. Stone has studied and compared vitamin C needs and productions in test animals and compared them to our needs. The findings are not absolute proof, but they suggest that a 150-pound human might need up to ten to fifteen grams of vitamin C when under stress.

Once we can see the whole picture everything becomes relatively simple and clear.

L. E. Orgel, another expert in protein chemistry, recently emphasized the importance of the maintenance of the accuracy of protein synthesis and its relevance to aging in a recent article in the Proceedings of the National Academy of Sciences (29).

Dr. Bjorksten is already fairly well advanced in his experimentation to undo cross-linking damage—his idea is basically very simple. First he takes old human brain tissue and dissolves everything except the large cross-linked molecules. Extraction and filtration leave only the large molecules as a residue. In the next step he searches for microorganisms that can attack these large molecules by developing specific enzymes. Then he isolates the new enzymes and purifies them. In the last step the new enzymes, when taken into our system, can undo the cross-links and REVERSE THE AGING PROCESS. By using old human brain tissue Dr. Bjorksten has already isolated large polymeric molecules, found organisms which develop specific enzymes that can attack these large molecules, and isolated and identified some of these enzymes.

CHAPTER 7

A Look at the Most Important Theories of Aging

Free Radical Theory of Aging
Cross-Link Theory
DNA—Damage Theory
Collagen Theory
Stress Theory
Mutation Theory
Metabolics Products Theory
Diffusion Theory
Immunologic Theory of Aging
Cybernetic Theory
Rate of Living Theory
Histone Theory
. . . and Suddenly the Picture Clears Up a Little.

We have seen in the previous chapters that many signs of aging are actually blamed as the cause of aging.

With an increase in age many changes take place:

Cell functions slow down; the DNA gets damaged; the RNA decreases in concentration; enzymes don't function as well any more; large molecules are formed at an increasing rate; brain functions slow down; and so on, and so on, and so on.

But all these are just signs of aging. What is the actual cause?

And here we have the most difficult question to answer. There are probably many different causes of aging, but three theories deal with the real causes of aging and deserve special attention: the "Free Radical

Theory", the "Cross-Link Theory" and the "Composite Theory of Aging." These theories actually show us why these changes take place and what causes these changes. At least we have solved a part of the riddle and, as Bjorksten has shown, it is not necessary to solve the entire problem. The prevention of only ten percent of all causes of aging could lead to an average life span of about 170 years.

Actually it is no longer a question of which theory is correct, because free radicals, the damaging effects of radicals, cross-linking, radiation, etc., are proven facts of aging. The only question is to what degree these factors contribute to aging. The other real concern here is what can be done about these facts.

When we talk about theories on aging, there are a few facts that nobody really doubts. One, for example, is the belief that the life span of any species is controlled by its genetic code. This "genetic clock" determines why dogs have a maximum life span of about 29 years, horses about 48 years and fruit flies only about 41 days. Some researchers believe that we all have "aging genes." But if this is true the question arises again: What actually gets these aging genes going? Free radicals maybe?

Let's now take a look at the different theories on aging.

The free radical theory on aging was already discussed in Chapter 5, the cross-link theory was discussed in Chapter 6 and the DNA damage theory was discussed in some detail in Chapter 3.

1) *The Collagen Theory*. This theory has been discussed in detail by F. Verzar. It holds that aging is due to the formation of cross-links between collagen molecules and fibrous proteins that support bone, tendon, cartilage and connective tissue. Over the years

these cross-linked collagen molecules shrink and strangle many healthy cells (25). Reactive free radicals and cross-linking agents are definitely responsible for part of the cross-links if not for all of them. It is easily demonstrated in a laboratory that free radicals and cross-linking agents form bonds between protein molecules.

The only other reasonable cause for bond formation between these molecules could be the action of an enzyme. This raises the question: Is this bond formation a planned aging process? Should it turn out that an enzyme is involved, it would not be difficult with our modern research equipment to identify it and to find a drug that deactivates it or counteracts its effects. In this case it would probably be easier to deactivate an enzyme than to synthesize an enzyme which will "undo" the links that have already been formed. The undoing of already existing bonds would have to be accomplished with a very specific enzyme that works only on these bonds, since every molecule contains many such "covalent bonds."

It is encouraging to know that researchers are working on both sides of the problem and are already obtaining good results from test animals.

2) *The Stress Theory of Aging*, as proposed by P. Prioreschi and H. Selye, states that the body and the cells can take a certain amount of stress but that we often put too much stress on the cells so that even the proper rest and the right nutrients cannot remove all the effects of the stress. This constant stress gradually wears out the cells and drives them to the point where they become completely worn out and where the division mechanism triggers off the cell division (4). This theory is of great importance but has not received enough attention, probably because it does not have an explanation for the cross-links between molecules.

Dr. Bjorksten's theory not only explains links but also agrees with the stress factor the clearly established that an excess stress on the makes them age faster than normal. Faulty nutrit. smoking (with the poisonous chemicals inhaled), a. pollution and an excessive amount of alcohol are the major stress factors that you should be concerned with, besides mental stress.

A physically untrained system is also more suscepti- ble to stress; thus lack of exercise constitutes another stress factor. Naturally other stress factors will be dis- covered, but you should take account of the basic stress factors first. The "hows and whys" are summar- ized in Chapters 4, 15, 16 and 17. There is more about stress, how it affects aging and what we can do about it in Chapter 18.

3) *The Mutation Theory* by L. Szilard, which has received much attention from scientists, states that the parts of the cells (78) which are characteristic to the body (mainly the DNA) undergo mutations. When these mutations occur repeatedly and are car- ried over into new cells, the DNA becomes less effi- cient. A schematic representation of this type of change was represented in Figure 4. This theory is absolutely correct but does not state what actually causes these mutations. Moreover, free radicals and cross-linking agents can explain the mutations. Among other experimenters who prove this point, H. J. Rhase has demonstrated that hydrogen peroxide, a compound which is responsible for radical formations, reacts with adenine (a DNA nucleotide) to change its structure (30, 31, 32, 33, 34).

This mutation theory also received special attention from J. W. Hart and D. Carpenter in their article "Toward an Integrated Theory of Aging," (35) which is another attempt to sum up the aging problem.

Dr. Curtice of Brookhaven National Laboratory has

animals that abnormal chromosomes
...hese animals age. Are these chromo-
...sponsible for the decrease of RNA in
...uite possible. As you remember, RNA
...DNA and it is reasonable to assume
...DNA produces less RNA than an un-

Chromosome damage is probably the primary cause
of aging even though this process is much more complicated than assumed at first.

Other researchers like Dr. Hahn in Switzerland
studied a group of compounds that are associated
with DNA. These compounds, called histones, cling
more strongly to the DNA in older animals than in
younger ones. But again, these stronger bonds could
be formed in some type of cross-linking.

4) *The Metabolic Products Theory* says that aging
is due to an accumulation of metabolic products
which are not excreted fast enough. This theory also
makes sense, but I would classify the excessive metabolic products as a stress factor.

In the light of this theory, the saying "don't burn
the candle at both ends" makes a lot of sense. You
have to be able to recognize how much your body can
take: there is a limit to everything. If you "overdo" almost any activity, your metabolic rate will be very
high and as a result your body will have trouble getting rid of all the oxidation products. If you are over-
worked and exhausted and still keep going, you will
get to a point where your efficiency decreases rapidly
and you just won't be able to go on. Sufficient rest
after being extremely active is an absolute necessity.
If you could rest with your body at a lower temperature so that your basic metabolic rate was lowered
even more, this would give your body an even better
chance to rid itself of the many oxidation products.
By sleeping in a relatively cool surrounding and not

stuffing yourself just before going to bed, the excretion of metabolic products improves tremendously.

5) *The Diffusion Theory* as proposed by D. G. Carpenter is a combination of the cross-link and the metabolic products theory. Both were discussed here previously (35).

6) *The Immunologic Theory* by R. L. Walford states that aging is due to decreasing immunologic reactions with age (36). Our body's defense mechanisms are of the utmost importance, and when their function diminishes with age, our body is left defenseless against even relatively harmless bacteria. Toxic materials are also not removed fast enough and all this wears out our cells at a faster and faster rate. Our defense mechanisms can also get a little confused and even attack our own body. As you will see, this theory fits very nicely into my overall view on aging. However, I would rather classify this diminution in defense mechanisms as a sign of aging and not as a cause of aging. What we have to do is to find out why our defense mechanisms diminish. If we want to prevent our defense mechanisms from attacking our own body, we can deactivate them with chemicals, but that leaves us completely defenseless against attack from the outside. There is however another method and that is to reactivate or rejuvenate our defensive systems. The researchers N. Fabris, W. Pierpaoli and E. Sorkin have recently extended the life expectancy of some dwarf mice from their normal three to five month life span to more than 12 months by reactivating their defense mechanisms with lymphocytes (140). There is more about results with immunosuppressants in Chapter 14.

7) *The Cybernetic Theory of Aging* by J. W. Still assumes that aging is due to an increasing loss of control of the nervous system over all functions of the body (37). Now if there is a loss of control, it must be

due to some kind of damage to the nervous system. It is often argued that nerve cells, especially since they do not divide, should be highly affected by radicals and cross-linking and break down at a faster rate.

Further, it is a fact that the chemical make-up of nerve cells is different from that of other cells. Hence it may be found that chemical difference of chemicals are the answer. If nerve cells are just ten to 20% more resistant against radicals or cross-linking agents, that could explain everything. Possibly one or more of the chemicals in our nerve cells acts as a radical scavenger and deactivates radicals.

8) *The Rate of Living Theory* of R. Pearl correlates surface area of tissue with energy expenditure in different animals and humans. It found that a relationship exists between the metabolic rate and the life span: a high metabolic rate causes a short life span and vice versa. It also found that this is due to the need to maintain a certain body temperature (38). This theory is quite correct and does not disagree with the combination theory. Accordingly, a life span increase could be obtained by decreasing our metabolic rate, and this might be achieved by lowering the body temperature during the rest period.

Researchers have already shown that the life span of coldblooded animals can be doubled by keeping these animals at a lower temperature, but it doesn't work with warmblooded animals. Dr. Walford at the University of California doubled the life span of fish by keeping these fish in a surrounding that was about five degrees colder than normal. Dr. Loeb, Dr. Northrop and Dr. Barrows showed that the same effect was obtained for fruit flies and rotifers.

Recently several attempts have been made to correlate the different aging theories. *Toward an Integrated Theory of Aging* is a fine paper by J. W. Hart and D. Carpenter (39). It is a bit different from what

I have outlined here and gives more detailed information on every aspect of aging. If you are scientifically inclined, you might consider this article for future reading. *Human Aging Research* by R. A. Passwater and P. A. Welker is another approach to solving the aging problem. This article is in my opinion a very practical and reasonable approach to the aging problem. In it, the authors have evaluated the possibilities of what you can do *today* to retard the aging process. Their research results are excellent and will be discussed in Chapter 14 (40).

If we now look back at all the different theories on aging we find that the decreased performance of our cells boils down to a damaged DNA, structurally changed other parts of the cell, an accumulation of oxidation products and stress in general.

Two of the factors that can cause the damage are already known—free radicals and cross-linking agents. It is now up to us to prevent the formation of these damaging species and to repair at least part of the damage that has been done already. We also know how to decrease stress factors.

My own theory on aging is not very different from the theories explained above; it actually is a combination of several theories and therefore I would like to call it "The Combination Theory On Aging." The reason for combining several theories is that I believe the only thing wrong with gerontology is that too many researchers are looking for the "one cause" of aging.

a) Since aging is an extremely complex process we have to view it at first in terms of cell losses and decreasing cell efficiencies and then, in the second step, determine why we lose cells and why the efficiency decreases.

b) The life span of any species is determined by the

death or strongly decreased efficiency of a critical number of cells of a major organ which causes the organ to cease its functions which in turn causes the organ system to terminate its functions etc.

c) The decrease of the efficiency and final death of cells is mainly due to

1) An increasing damage to the DNA with time which causes a decreasing effectiveness of the DNA as the substance which controls everything.

2) A decrease in the DNA-repair mechanism with age.

3) A decreasing effectiveness of enzymes.

4) A decreasing control of enzyme reactions due to lower hormone concentrations.

5) Large molecules in the cells which increase with age and are not body characteristic.

6) Other reasons (not yet discovered).

d) The possible causes of these cellular malfunctions and changes are:

1) Free radicals.

2) Cross linking agents other than free radicals.

3) Enzymes that accelerate aging.

4) A decrease of the immunologic system with age which puts more stress on all cells.

5) Drugs, toxic materials and other stress factors which interfere with normal cellular processes.

6) Other reasons (not yet discovered).

Most of the causes mentioned above under d) are accelerated by an accumulation of oxidation products in the cells, caused by over-exertion of the system or malfunctions of the cellular excretory system.

e) The maximum possible life span for humans under optimum conditions is at least 120 to 140 years, determined to some degree genetically. The major areas that prevent humans from reaching this maximum possible life span are faulty nutrition, lack of exercise, smoking, excessive use of alcohol, air pollution, stress and a negative attitude towards life. All these areas are synergistic; they enhance each other. For example: if the average loss of years is 9 years for smoking, 7 years for lack of exercise and 12 years for excessive use of alcohol, a person that does all these things wrong will not lose an average of 28 years but at least 31 years. the more areas are violated, the more dramatic is the loss of years. Smoking and lack of exercise are highly synergistic. Extending our life span past the possible maximum of 120 to 140 years is possible by preventing the causes of cellular malfunctions. That means the more causes we identify and learn to prevent, the longer our life span will get and maybe some day we will be able to live forever.

As you can see, my theory combines several theories on aging but the most important fact is that there is no single cause of aging. Many factors working independent of each other make us age.

CHAPTER 8

Other Aging Factors

*Why is Shirali Mislimov 167 years old, still
working and fit enough to ride his horse?*
                    Or
*Due to smoking, air pollution, lack of exercise,
and alcohol you might loose an average of 25
years of your life.*

Not very long ago newspapers throughout the
world reprinted a *Tass* report on the 101st wedding
anniversary of a Russian couple living in the hamlet
of Ilkhychi. At the ages of 130 and 114 they were an
extremely healthy and good-looking couple. The hamlet of Ilkhychi is situated on the Caspian sea, an area
well known for its long-living inhabitants (41). Another area where the average life expectancy is far
above the world's average is Arachova on Mount Par-
nassus in Greece. In the province of Azebaijan in the
USSR 84 out of 10,000 live over 100 years (42).
Studies such as these should reveal some information
about the maximum human life span. The Bastions of
Longevity as Dr. Leaf defines them are Vilcamba in
Ecuador, the area of Hunza in Pakistani—controlled
Kashmi and Abkhazia in the southern Soviet Union.
(153).

The Russians also claim that in the area of
Abkhasia three out of every 1000 persons are over 100
years old. The USSR is also proud of its oldest person,
Shirali Mislimov. He is 167 years old; his wife is a
young kid of 120. He has never been sick, and he is

still working as a farmer and rides his horse for exercise. Here in the U.S. we have Mr. Lewis who is 105 years old, runs six miles per day and is extremely mentally alert.

Biologists have always insisted that the life span of a person is genetically fixed; that is, it could be an hereditary trait of the people living in these specific geographical areas. Heredity definitely plays an important role but is quite often over-emphasized. For example, take two people with different family medical histories. In the first's family many died of cancer, while only a few died of cancer in the second's family. Now if the first takes precautions, follows a plan of good nutrition and doesn't smoke, while the second doesn't worry about nutrition and smokes two packs of cigarettes per day, then the latter will definitely have a much higher chance of getting cancer regardless of his genetic code.

But now let's get back to the old people discussed above. If you examine the habits and life style of these people, you will find that they live extremely healthy and active lives. The people in the province of Azebaijan, for example, never drink alcohol or smoke, are physically active and never overeat (42). They seem satisfied with their lives, don't worry about financial or emotional problems as much as we do, and don't find it necessary to quarrel with each other. Their caloric intake is very low (approximately 1700 calories a day).

The social and economic pressures on older people in most western countries don't exist for these people. In these areas old people are honored and respected and always consulted when important decisions have to be made. Since they are needed, they don't feel that they are a burden to anyone. As a result, STRESS is at a minimum; and these people are living proof of Dr. Selye's theory on aging (discussed in Chapters 7, 19 and 20).

Biologists have also projected our possible maximum life span as being between 120 and 130 years. The reason why you don't live to that age is two-fold: Many lives are terminated before that time due to illnesses; and habits or life style are, on the average, anything but healthy. We make tremendous mistakes in the areas of nutrition, exercise, smoking and drinking alcohol. You can even protect yourself well against air pollution. The importance of the above-mentioned areas cannot be emphasized enough. If you do not know how important exercise is, or how hazardous the effect of smoking and air pollution are in relation to health and aging, you can read up on the facts in Chapters 16, 17, and 18. However, to do something about the above-mentioned topics is almost a prerequisite for taking youth compounds. You could extend YOUR specific life expectancy without doing something about the above-mentioned topics, but statistics show that you could feel *much* better and even extend your life expectancy further by acting reasonably in the areas just mentioned.

Let's examine a few "efficiency curves" (Figure 1). Curve A shows the approximate "efficiency" of a person who does everything wrong in the above-mentioned areas. His efficiency curve is very low and his average life expectancy is short. The physical and mental performance of such a person is extremely low compared to what it could be (curve B). If person "A" starts taking youth compounds that slow down the aging process, he (or she) will obviously be able to extend his life span and obtain a new efficiency curve—A-plus. But since the physical and mental performance have already become very low, I have serious doubts that this person will be able to enjoy his extra years; he will merely drag on.

On the other hand, a person who does almost everything right in every area (again, you don't have to become a health nut) and keeps his performance curve as high as possible will definitely enjoy his longer life span (curve B-plus). Studies have shown that a medium-to-good exercise program (two 2 hour sessions per week, including jogging), raises your efficiency tremendously (and that includes your sexual performance) and adds between six to nine years to your average life expectancy (42, 43, 44).

Smoking has a dramatic effect on your mental alertness and sexual performance besides cutting down on your average life expectancy. Inhaling too much carbon monoxide can also do serious damage to your brain. If you are a heavy smoker you can deactivate ten to 15% of your blood due to carbon monoxide inhalation. As a result the oxidation in your system also decreases and oxidation products that cause cross-linking are formed in a higher percentage. Smoking therefore makes you age faster, and there is a good chance that the large amounts of carbon monoxide bring you a big step closer to senility. For a heavy smoker, the decrease in the average life expectancy is 8.3 years (45).

Air pollution also decreases the average life span. Since people are constantly moving from one geographical locale to another, it is difficult to carry out precise studies. However, a person who lives all his life in an area of very high air pollution can expect to lose approximately 5 to 8 years of his life. This is a very rough estimate since sufficient data are not yet available. If you live in the center of a highly poluted area like Los Angeles, New York, or the South Side of Chicago, the loss of years is probably even higher.

Good nutrition is an absolute must. I don't even have to argue that point. Since it is difficult to say where bad nutrition starts, it is also difficult to say when. What is bad nutrition? Three slices of bread with jelly per day? One cup of coffee and toast for breakfast and a salad later in the day? You don't believe that's possible? Just ask a model what she eats in order to stay "slim and beautiful." I believe that bad nutrition can take off approximately six to ten years of your average life span and I feel that this is a rather conservative estimate.

The high priority of physical and psychological stress is well established but sufficient data are not available to make precise estimates. An evaluation of the relative importance of stress, compared to other factors suggests that the average person loses approximately 5 to 9 years due to stress.

Alcohol abuse (five or more strong drinks per day) can decrease your life expectancy by another six to ten years (113).

So you can see that air pollution, smoking, lack of exercise, bad nutrition, stress and alcohol can take from 34 to 58 years of your possible life span.

For all other causes (illnesses, etc.) we allow an average loss of 10 to 15 years.

And here comes the final test: Let's add the loss of years due to *all* causes to the present average life expectancy and we should come out with the maximum possible life span for humans. Let's do it: average life span (71 years) plus loss of years due to all causes (minimum 42 years, maximum 68 years) gives us a maximum possible life span of 113 to 139 years. I must admit that these estimates are very rough, but isn't it impressive how close the numbers come to the maximum human life span estimated by biologists?

Since you want to stay mentally alert, you also want to stay away from drugs like LSD, etc. Recent studies have shown that chromosome and brain damage are definite risks for drug users (80). Even marijuana isn't as harmless as your neighborhood junky might tell you. In a recent study, a team of British researchers linked brain damage to heavy marijuana smoking (79). Dr. A. Campbell of the Bristol Royal United Hospitals and his associates have also shown that the regular use of marijuana can cause cerebral atrophy. A team of Philadelphia psychiatrists, Dr. W. T. Moore and Dr. H. Kolansky, confirmed these findings (154).

But what is more harmful, smoking cigarettes, smoking marijuana or drinking alcohol? Well, let me put it this way: I would rather see my friends smoking some marijuana than smoking 20 cigarettes per day or getting drunk twice a week.

A new set of rules or "How to treat people you don't like:"

If they smoke: Buy them cigarettes whenever possible; with the highest tar and nicotine content. Don't let any occasion pass without sending them your little nicotine presents. Tell them about your uncle who smoked 50 cigarettes per day and lived to be 49 . . . excuse me, 94.

If they are hungry: Take them to a place where "high in fats and carbohydrates" is the rule of the house. The later at night, the bigger and fatter the meal should be. In the morning buy them sweet rolls and donuts; tell them that eggs are no good because they contain cholesterol and cottage cheese and ham are much too fattening.

If they are thirsty: Take them to the nearest bar and buy them as much hard liquor as their heart desires. If they don't drink, any sweet soda will do. Tell them that red wine with mineral water makes a person sleepy and that orange and grapefruit juice are not good because they don't contain enough sugar.

Between meals: Have candy bars and other sweets available for them at any time.

If they had an argument or fight with somebody:

Work out a revenge plan with them; get their adrenalin flowing whenever you can. Be a real chum. Now remember, these were rules on how to treat people you DON'T like.

CHAPTER 9

Sex and Aging

Dr. Leaf asked the old people in the Caucasus to what age they thought youth extends. I quote: "Quada Jonashian, age 110, also of Gulripshi, was embarrassed at the question, since I was accompanied by a woman doctor from the regional health center. He thought "youth" meant engaging in sexual activity and admitted that he had considered himself a youth until a dozen years ago."

National Geographic
January 1973

I remember a day quite clearly when several of us students were sitting in the university cafeteria and discussing a chemistry problem in detail. One girl, who lived off campus with her parents in order to keep her cost of living down, didn't participate in our conversation. Instead she sat there with a glorified smile on her face and seemed to be quite far away in her thoughts. "Hey Sue, what nice things are you thinking about," I asked. Still in some kind of daze, she replied, "You know I am living with my parents. My room is directly under my parent's bedroom and our old house is not very soundproof. My father is 64 and my mother is 59 and about twice a week I can hear the old bedsprings squeaking and moving. Last night the old stud was at it again, twice in one night, at about 10:30 and again at 12. To hear that gives me a really good feeling and I know why they are such a happy couple." We were all thinking our own thoughts and only Heinz, a foreign student at the Univeristy, commented: "Ja, ja, chemistry iss verrry interresstink."

Whenever the question about sex and older people comes up, a lot of people seem quite reluctant to talk about it. Why is that so? We might find the answer when we examine what some people think about sex during old age. When my colleagues conducted an informal interview with a large group of people between the ages of 50 and 80, a number of typical and often wrong statements were made. Let's examine a few of them.

"Sex makes you age faster." W R O N G! There is absolutely no evidence that sex accelerates the aging process. To the contrary, doctors believe that sex in old age has a highly stimulating and somehow rejuvenating effect. Sexually active people are normally happier, more relaxed and less willing to fight about every little thing. The state of mind of an older person is extremely important. Who do you think lives a happier retirement, a person who sits at home in a rocking chair awaiting the end of his life or somebody who goes out on dates and enjoys all his free time by continuing the old game of conquest and love? The desire for sex decreases a little bit with old age but this is often due to the person's attitude. Some people just give up too easily.

"Sex is bad for your heart" is another completely wrong statement. Sex is actually a good exercise for staying in shape and is improved dramatically by doing exercises and staying physically fit. Watching your weight, doing all kinds of exercises that you like and getting enough rest and good nutrition have improved many an oldster's sexual performance. Think of the sex organ as a muscle. If you keep it in good

shape by exercising, it will pe
when a person does not have sex f
a year or longer) the desire for se
pear completely, and some people (
have problems restarting it again. So
give up too easily, but most of the time
result in permanent damage. A consultatio
doctor and an understanding partner w
what to do will cure the problem. To preve
currence of this problem, when a partner is f
reason not available for the sex act, doctors r
mend masturbation to keep everything in good sl

"I just can't find a suitable partner; young girls j
don't like older men" said one 68-year-old man. Th
man's problem is only that he doesn't try hard
enough. Naturally if he is trying to find a 20-year-old
girl, he might have some problem, even though there
are many old men with very young girl friends. Some
young girls prefer the understanding, security and
knowledge of an older man to the attentions of a pen-
niless boy who doesn't know how to handle a woman.
More likely a man of his age would look for a partner
who is a little closer to his age. Older women have as
much sex drive as old men. After menopause, hormones in a woman's system change a little and
women become slightly less sensitive which reduces
the desire for sex. But this is no problem because
there are creams that contain estrogens which can increase the sensitivity.

Sex is mainly psychological; some doctors say as
much as 90%. So, if a 65-year-old man has sex problems and a physical examination shows that nothing is
wrong, the first thing doctors try to find is if he has
any "hang up." People very often talk themselves into
believing that there is something wrong with them; a
problem that occurs with older people as much as it
does with young people.

n young people often be-
ctive or even completely
have a very active sex
ey believe that they
their whole life, so
e young, they will
All this is com-
. Actually, the
that had a good
also have a good sex

at other sex problems older
ncounter. This is to show older
ething can be done and to show young-
that there can be sex, and a lot of it, in
ge.

Sometimes middle-aged or older men have problems with enlarged prostate glands. The prostate
gland consists of three lobes near the bladder and the
urethra. In many cases it causes discomfort and has to
be removed. The removal of this gland does not mean
that you lose your sexual powers; rather, it actually
improves sexual performance in many cases. Further,
it is not classified as a dangerous operation.

If a man has problems achieving a full erection,
there is also hope from medicine. A small elastic rod
can be inserted into the penis, which again is not a
complicated procedure. I know that it sounds awful
to have a silicon polymer inserted into the penis, but
it works pretty well and has made many men (and
women, too) happy.

For the treatment of cancer of the prostate, men
are sometimes given female hormones, but this can
lead to impotence for as long as the patient is under
treatment.

Even though there are only very few older women
"on the pill," the number of women that do take the

pill seems to increase. Not considering the side effects that some pills show, an older woman should actually feel a little better if she is on the pill since it adds hormones to her system.

Talking percentages, there is only a very small number of "legitimate" causes for not being sexually active. Some of them are the removal of the sex organs due to cancer and the formation of large plaques directly under the penis (called peyronies disease), or if a person is on high blood pressure pills, or if for other reasons the blood flow to the penis is blocked. There are 50-year-old men who are inactive and there are 92-year-old men who still have intercourse frequently. There is no actual age limit for having or not having intercourse.

There are studies available that show that sex around the age of 100 is nothing unusual if a person is healthy and physically fit; even after the age of 100 having children is no impossibility (109, 110).

Live sperms are produced by man for an average of about 70 years. Even though a man ceases to produce live sperm, his potency will often continue and a good sex life is possible. The present "average" man is not considered a very healthy specimen; living a healthy life and doing almost everything right in the different areas would increase performances dramatically and permit a good sex life up to at least 90 or 100 years. As of today approximately 70% of the people around the age of 70 years have sexual intercourse; what would that percentage be if their efficiency curves in general were twice as high?

Male impotence in older age: mainly (about 90%) psychological. Sexual failures which occur only sometimes and are quite normal often start a man worrying about himself. "What's wrong with me?" he asks. This kind of thinking, especially before the next sexual encounter, can start off a whole chain reaction. Often a wrong partner who doesn't understand the situation or doesn't have a good feeling for a good sexual relationship can accelerate this process. Hormones are used and can help but the main thing is to get the head straightened out. Try a little self-brain-washing: stand in front of a mirror and tell yourself: you are great, you can handle any situation, any woman. You must start believing in yourself.

UNHAPPY WITH YOUR SEX LIFE? OR JUST WANT TO IMPROVE IT?

Even though sex, or making love, is a very emotional thing and is mainly up in your head, your body plays an important role in it, and there are a few simple rules you should follow if you want to get the maximum out of it:

1) "Super-nutrition" is of number one importance again. Don't stuff yourself shortly before going to bed. A constant blood sugar level isn't only important for excellent thinking and working.

2) Make sure you are well exercised. If you are physically fit and not overweight you will be a better lover. Don't try to do everything at the same time, for example going through a good workout and immediately afterwards trying to set records with your wife or husband, girl friend or boy friend. Give your body a chance to rest up after exercise; make sure that you always get enough rest.

3) Don't take sexual failures too seriously. Illness, faulty nutrition, stress, a bad mood, the wrong partner and many other factors can seriously affect your body's functioning.

4) Are you at peace with yourself and your sexual attitude? Make sure your head is straight in respect to sex and other things.

5) Are you compatible with your partner? Do you

turn each other on? Or is sex like a cup of luke-warm coffee that doesn't even have the right flavor? Advice is hard to give; you will have to evaluate the situation yourself.

6) The compounds you might be taking to slow down the aging process should improve both your health and your sex life, but they definitely shouldn't affect your sexual performance in a negative way.

7) If a partner is not available for an extended time, masturbate from time to time. Be careful with mechanical devices like vibrators, etc. A woman might get so accustomed to the fast and highly stimulating movements of these devices that it is impossible for her to get full satisfaction from her lover.

8) Hormones are used with good results in older or exhausted people to get the sex organs functioning better again. However, when you stop taking the hormones, the effects of the hormones are also reduced again. Our goal is therefore to revitalize the organs that make the sex hormones instead of just adding these hormones to our system. However, hormones could be quite helpful in keeping our bodies functioning better in old age. As explained in Chapter 4, there are many different hormones that act as messengers in the control of our body functions. Since almost every hormone decreases with age, it would be reasonable to suggest to add hormones in such quantities to bring their concentration back to normal. This sounds good, but is not that easy. Hormones seem to work together in controlling the body functions and there is good evidence that we haven't even discovered all the hormones yet. The recent discovery of a thymus hormone, thymosin, is such an example. It was also found that this hormone decreases with age and that added thymosine might help to keep our immunologic system functioning longer. Dr. A. Goldstein of the University of Texas, Galveston, has worked with this

hormone extensively and found that when mice were injected with thymosine, their immunity increased (150). If we could revitalize our immunologic system with this hormone, this would definitely mean an improvement in health and longevity.

But hormone treatments also have their drawbacks. Some researchers believe that there is enough evidence that for example long term treatment with sex hormones can cause cancer. I personally believe that this fear is much overdone, but nobody has real proof.

A good hormone treatment would include treatment with several hormones. That means that at first a deviation from the normal level would have to be determined. In the second step we could make up the difference with synthetic or animal hormones.

But wouldn't it be better to revitalize all the organs that produce hormones instead of adding hormones? That's exactly what we are trying to do in one experiment with animals. By injecting RNA from these organs we hope to revitalize the hormonal system. The animals are doing all right but it is to early to talk about these experiments.

There are a few doctors that use hormones extensively with good results, they claim. Hormone treatment makes sense but as of this day we just don't know enough to influence effectively and slow down the aging process. I believe that when we start combining several hormones in hormone treatments, we will see better results.

If you still believe that something should be done about your sex life you might consider organ specific nucleic acids (Chapter 11). They are better than hormone treatments, but only available in Germany. Cell shots (also Chapter 11) are also used in Europe to treat sex problems. However, statistical data showing the effectiveness of these treatments are not available.

Sex is also a good way to lose weight or just to maintain your present weight and keep fit. We have a saying in Germany: "Ein guter Hahn wird selten fett," which means: a good rooster seldom gets fat. This is quite true and if this is one of the ways you want to keep yourself in shape you might want to read more about it in Dr. A. Friedman's book *How Sex Can Keep You Slim*. Dr. Friedman's formula for losing weight in bed (or wherever you do these things) reads as follows:

$$\frac{(Sn + 200) \times Sx}{2,400} = \text{weight loss in pounds.}$$

Where Sn stands for the number of calories contained in a snack that you don't eat because you'd rather make love (Sx = number of times you make love). The formula is not very precise and will give you only an approximate idea of how much weight you might lose. In order to be more precise, the formula should contain two other correction factors for vigor and time because you all know (I hope) there is making love and there is MAKING LOVE!!!!! Kavrooom.

Also, if a man wants to lose weight by making love, he might need some help from his doctor since overweight men often have a low concentration of sex hormones (111). This might explain why overweight people have a decreased sex drive and resort to eating and drinking.

But sex is actually not the way to get into shape and, especially if you want to be good at love-making, physical fitness is almost a must. In other words: you don't make love in order to get in shape, you exercise and keep fit in order to be a better lover.

CHAPTER 10

Youth Surgery

From the standpoint of biology, surgery doesn't really slow down aging—still, it can make a person look and feel years younger. A more youthful and appealing look can change a born pessimist into an optimist, and an introvert into an extrovert. "You are as old as you feel" is more than a truism. A 30 minute operation, undergone as an outpatient, can make a person look ten to 15 years younger, and more appealing.

Imagine a woman or a man who has seldom received more than a first glance from the opposite sex. Then, after a short operation, the whole world suddenly recognizes that they are there and smiles at them. What a morale booster! When a nondescript person whom nobody seemed to recognize changes into a person whose presence is appreciated everywhere, that person will also be changed into a much-happier human being. When you feel happy your whole outlook is changed and you also feel younger and more vigorous. If you can have all this for 500 dollars and maybe a week of seclusion, why shouldn't you take advantage of it?

Recently a friend of mine had her nose straightened a little. My first thought, when she told me about it on the phone, was "Why did she do it"? She was such an absolutely gorgeous creature, with a beautiful body and a perfect set of legs, that you just wouldn't think about her nose not being absolutely straight (though very often a person is conscious

about such minor details). ...
bothered her a lot; so she finally ...
and had her nose straightened. An ...
To do something like this it takes a ...
feeling for beauty. The new nose must fi...
is not just a question of performing good...
That's actually how I was introduced to D...
whom I have to thank for advice on this chapt...

But now let's get down to the nitty gritty det...
and answer the following questions: What types o...
youth surgery are there? Is it painful? How much does
it cost? How long will you want to hide from your surroundings? How long (if at all) will you have to stay
in a hospital?

Let's start with the nose. As a person grows older,
his nose grows longer. So if you have your nose shortened by the removal of some material under the
skin, you will look younger. The procedure is almost
the same as for straightening a nose. All of these operations are literally painless because you are under
partial or full sedation. The operation can be undergone as an outpatient, but in order that you may feel
more at ease a stay of one or two days in the hospital
is recommended. The price ranges from $500 to $1000
depending on what has to be done. Shopping around
a little also helps. If you pay more, that definitely
doesn't mean that your doctor is better. After the operation you will feel a little uncomfortable for a few
days since you have to wear a small brace over the
nose. This is just to protect the new masterpiece until
it is less sensitive to touch and irritation. You will
want to hide for about one week. That is how long
you should wear the brace.

Removal of *bags* and *wrinkles* under and around
the *eyes*, the *chin* and the *forehead*. Each single operation is again a very short operation, is not painful
and will cost you about $500 to $1000. People often

parts of their face done at
[bi]nation surgery costs ap-
three days in the hospital,
two weeks and you are

forehead) requires a lit-
days in the hospital and
[fr]iends after about two to
[a]pproximately $1500 to

[si]mple lift," where small incisions
made on the side of the head under the hairline
in order to pull up the whole face a little, is not performed very often. Actually this is not a very good
method because the skin stretches again and soon you
are back where you started.

Removal of *scars* and the effects of *severe acne*.
The "sandpaper surgery" which is used to remove
scars from the skin is actually done with a very fast
rotating diamond-studded wheel. The overall effect is
a smoothing out of the surface of the skin. Larger
scars are cut out at first, sewn up and later smoothed
out with the wheel. This procedure can be undergone
as an outpatient but since some people are very nervous about these things they normally stay in the hospital for about two days.

To have a scar removed you will pay between $150
and $450, and the abrasion process will cost between
$75 and $250.

This procedure doesn't really work well in the removal of small wrinkles.

Breast surgery and *silicones*. In some countries silicone injections are performed where silicone fluids
are injected under the skin of the breasts to give
them the desired shape. This procedure is against the
law in the U.S. since it was found that these silicones
can move in the body and cause serious damage.

A method used in the U.S. that does not show these effects is the use of silicone gel implants which are inserted under the skin to give a fullness to the breasts. This type of surgery is quite common and is performed about 300 times per year in a city like Chicago. The prosthesis (implants) costs about $250 and the surgery runs from $750 to $1500. You will want to stay in the hospital for three to five days and then you will have a feeling of tightness in the breasts for about two weeks, similar to the feeling of tightness a woman often has during her period. You won't have to keep off sexual activity for more than ten to 14 days.

Correction of *protruding ears*. This type of surgery is extremely fast and requires only very small incisions. The cost is about $400 to $700. It can be undergone as an outpatient, but to prevent any damage from tossing around during sleep, patients stay in the hospital for about two days.

Chemical surgery for the skin. In this process a solution containing mainly phenol is applied to the surface of the skin which removes the top layer of the skin and the wrinkles with it. Tapes cover the treated areas for about one to two days. The layer of skin below is new and younger looking. This method is mainly used to remove wrinkles around the mouth and the eyes. The cost is about $250 to $750. Few doctors actually use this method, not because they love scalpels more than chemicals but because this treatment leaves lines between the treated and untreated skin which you have to cover up with makeup.

Before somebody comes up with the statement "chemical surgery kills people," let me clarify this point. Phenol is a strong chemical and it has to be used as such. There was a time when some "beauty experts" tried to do the phenol treatment step by step by using dilute solutions. However, when a dilute solution was used it was found that the phenol was absorbed through the skin and slowly poisoned the patient. This area is well researched and there is no danger that you might get killed by chemical surgery.

Hair transplants. In this procedure punches or strips of hair are taken from the back of the head and transplanted to the front or top. It is best done when there is still enough hair to cover the spots where the transplants were performed, because it takes about five months from the time of the transplant until about two inches of hair have grown. It will take about 12 to 15 dots on each side to fill in small corners. About 20 to 30 dots are transplanted at a time and the cost ranges from $8 to $15 per dot. If you don't have enough hair to cover the transplants you will probably wear a toupe for a few months or cover your head otherwise. When hair transplants are done, the first dots cannot be very close because the blood supply to the transplants would decrease. Therefore hair transplants are often done in two steps. The first set of dots is spread far apart and a few months later other transplants are made to fill in the spaces.

Phyllis Diller provides an example of a well-done face-lift. If you saw her on the television show that showed pictures of her before and after the surgery, you were stunned by the difference. I think everybody who saw the difference will agree that she looked at least 20 years younger.

PART III

Extending Our Life Expectancy— What Have Researchers Come Up With?

Many researchers are working on slowing down the aging process. If we put all the research results together, we come to the conclusion that as of today our life expectancy could be more than 120 healthy years.

CHAPTER 11

From Fresh Cell Therapy To Regeneresen

1530: Heart heals heart,
Spleen heals spleen,
Kidney heals kidney.

                              PARACELSUS.

1973: Heart RNA heals heart,
Spleen RNA heals spleen,
Kidney RNA heals kidney.

Back in 1930 a young doctor named Paul Niehans was working on grafting animal tissue on to human organs. He became quite successful and well known in his field. In a hospital in Bern, Switzerland a woman was operated on, and trouble developed with her parathyroid gland. All therapeutic measures failed, and the only chance of saving her life was to get a parathyroid gland transplant from an animal. The woman was therefore transferred to Dr. Niehans' hospital. When she arrived, Dr. Niehans recognized that it was too late for a transplant since the patient was dying. In a last effort Dr. Niehans chopped up the parathyroid gland of a steer, mixed these "minced" parathyroid gland cells in a salt and water solution and injected them into the muscles of the patient. To the surprise of the entire medical profession, the muscle spasms went away and the patient recovered completely. The injected cells had actually performed the duties of the damaged gland, and this was the birth of "fresh cell therapy."

After more research it was found that whenever

cells from animal or human embryos were injected into the muscles of an older or exhausted person, there was a highly rejuvenating effect. However, if the cells were taken from animals or humans *some time* after birth, a violent rejection of the cells occurred. It was therefore believed that cells develop their own specific characteristics after birth and that only cells of unborns could be used for cell therapy. It was also observed that cells from specific organs (again from embryos) could improve the same organs in an adult when injected into the muscles. "Treat Like With Like," as the saying goes. Liver problems were treated with liver cells, heart diseases were treated with heart cells, and even the impotence of middle-aged and exhausted businssmen was treated with cells from testes (46, 47, 48).

The reasons for the success of this rejuvenating process is still a mystery. It seems as if Professor Niehans stumbled onto something "big before its time" but recognized the high value of his findings. Since his initial experimentation with fresh cell therapy, Professor Paul Niehans has treated international figures, including Pope Pius XII who appointed him to the chair of the Pontifical Academy of Sciences in 1955.

In the light of our modern DNA theories we can come up with three possible mechanisms for cell therapy. In Chapter 3 we learned that young, undamaged cells perform their duties perfectly. The DNA, RNA, mitochondria and enzymes in a young cell are undamaged and full of life generating forces.

Several mechanisms have been proposed as accounting for the rejuvenating effect of these cell injections. Two of the less likely are:

1) Whenever cells are injected they can travel as "whole cells" to the different parts of our body where they can live and contribute perfect cell products, restore cell reserves and help repair any damage.

2) A second possibility is that the cells disintegrate after injection and that only the mitochondria travel through our fluid system. Remember, the mitochondria are the small bodies in the cytoplasm that have to do with the energy conversions in the cells. It is believed that the mitochondria and the nucleus of the cells were two separate units at one time and that they first went into a type of symbiosis and then grew together to form a higher organism, the cell. Could be, because the mitochondria is quite an independent organelle with its own DNA.

A more plausible explanation for fresh cell rejuvenation is that the entire cells disintegrate and make all the basic, undamaged cell products available for older cells of our body. The embryonic cells contain all materials necessary to make new cells; everything, from enzymes to the DNA, is present in the right quantities and ratios.

Cell therapy is still a controversial method for two basic reasons:

1) Since we don't really know the mechanism of this rejuvenation, a doctor is very reluctant to use it, especially when it comes to injecting animal cells into our system.

2) There are not enough statistical data from humans available to show that it has a long-term effect rather than a very short temporary effect. This is partly due to the reluctance of the persons who had cell shots to make themselves available for long-term observations.

Cell therapy is a great discovery. However it can be improved to give even better results. Any long-term effect is probably due to an improved cell formation. The different compounds from the embryonic cells are incorporated into our cells at a very fast rate; actually this process sometimes takes just minutes. Even though millions of cells divide every day, the relative percentage that divide while the embryonic materials are available is very small. So actually only a very small part of our body is rejuvenated. If rejuvenated new cells are the cause of overall rejuvenation, then a much better effect should be obtained if not just one but several cell injections were performed within a certain time period. That again would be very expensive.

But there is another possibility. It might be better to use dried cell preparations more than once instead of real cells once; that could cut down on costs.

In his book about cell therapy, *The Secret of Eternal Youth*, Peter Stephan claims that numerous celebrities have undergone cell therapy but are reluctant to admit it. The names range from Marlene Dietrich, Charlie Chaplin and Gloria Swanson to the late President Eisenhower and German Chancellor Adenauer.

In order to give you a view from the top on this subject, I have asked Professor H. Hoepke, one of the top men in this field, to explain cell therapy in his own words. Professor Hoepke's views on cell therapy and aging you will find in Chapter 20.

There are, however, several informative books and scientific publications available that describe the fascinating topic of cell therapy and that might be of interest to the general reader. (46, 47, 48, 77).

Fresh cell therapy is used quite often in European countries. Just pick up a German newspaper and you will find many doctors advertising clinics that specialize in this field.

Somewhat similar to fresh cell therapy is a newer method of treatment with so-called REGENERESEN. Regeneresen are organ-specific ribonucleic acids which are injected intramuscularly.

But first a little background on this new treatment:

Several workers have shown that ribonucleic acids are necessary for the protein synthesis in our body.

We have already seen in Chapter 6 how important it is to maintain a good protein synthesis in our body and what can happen if missynthesized or malformed proteins are formed. It was shown that in cultures where the RNA was destroyed the protein synthesis stopped completely. When RNA, specific for this culture was added, the protein synthesis started again. With the help of the RNA the amino acids are connected with each other to give proteins. It was further shown that the protein synthesis can be increased up to 100% with added, organ-specific RNS (95, 96, 97, 98).

But what does this have to do with the aging process? Burger and Heyden found that the RNA concentration starts to decrease in humans after the age of 40 (102, 103). Decreased RNA concentration—decreased protein synthesis—means decreased efficiency of the entire system. If we now add organ-specific RNA to our system we can normalize the protein synthesis again. That the RNAs are organ-specific was shown by Cachin, Pergola, Brux and Brun in an interesting experiment. They treated animals and humans that had liver damage with two different RNAs, namely unspecific yeast RNA and organ-specific RNA. While the improvement with yeast RNA was small, the improvement was 60% with the organ-specific RNA (99).

We pointed out earlier that learning and memory are closely connected with protein synthesis (100). Davidson, Davis, Cook, Green and Fellows demonstrated that the learning process in animals is dramatically increased when organ-specific RNA is injected (101).

In Russia the scientists Kalcin, Polezhaev and Solnoeava induced heart muscle damage in dogs and treated these dogs with heart muscle RNA. The dogs recovered completely. The heart RNA obviously improved the heart protein synthesis which led to a complete repair of the damage (104).

Professor H. Dyckerhoff specialized in this area and developed several RNA combinations. The one that is of great importance for the rejuvenation of older persons is a preparation called RN-13. This RN-13 preparation contains RNA from 13 different organs. When injected, the added RNAs can catalyze the synthesis of proteins and bring it back to normal. The overall effect is a rejuvenation of the entire body. I would definitely prefer this treatment to any hormone treatment because it is more reasonable to rejuvenate the organs that produce the hormones than just to add hormones to our system (105, 106).

Professor Dyckerhoff also developed several treatments of diseases with organ-specific ribonucleic acids. Paracelsus said: heart heals heart, spleen heals spleen and kidney heals kidney. Now we know a little better why this is so and, in order to be more precise, we could say: heart RNA heals heart, spleen RNA heals spleen and kidney RNA heals kidney.

There are RNA treatments for about 80 diseases which range from Addison's disease, atheroscleroses, impotence, frigidity, heart trouble, leukemia and hearing problems to sterility (107).

These ribonucleic acid preparations are sold in Germany under the name "Regeneresen."

Let me summarize:

a) We know that the maintenance of a good protein synthesis is of the utmost importance for our physical and mental well-being.

b) Organ-specific RNA is necessary for a good protein synthesis.

c) It was established that the RNA decreases after the age of 40.

d) In older age the protein synthesis can be improved by adding organ-specific RNA to our system.

e) Organ-specific RNAs can also be used in any age group to treat diseases that are connected to a faulty protein synthesis.

In my own experiments I use a combination of different organ-specific nucleic acids from 13 major organs (RN-13). As of this date, several experiments in which we are trying to extend the average life expectancy of test animals (mice and rats) look very good but it is too early to evaluate any results. There are, however, some other experiments worth mentioning.

1) Twelve white mice, aged ten months, in three adjacent cages had caught some virus or other disease. The animals didn't move around, ate and drank only very little and got worse every day. I separated them into two groups and gave each mouse in one group an injection of 0.3 mg of organ-specific nucleic acids and repeated this injection two days later. Five of the six mice that received that injection recovered. All six mice in the other group that didn't get the injections died.

2) Rats that are used for breeding are normally retired after five litters because the number of offspring in each litter sharply decreases after this time. Working with retired breeders, we were able to increase the litter size by about 25% by giving these old animals RN-13 injections.

Dr. Benjamin Frank has worked with oral doses of RNA and DNA in this country and deserves credit for this pioneering work (discussed in Chapter 14).

3) Snell-Bagg dwarf mice have a short life span of three to five months. They age much faster than the normal Snell-Bagg mice which have a life expectancy of about 18 months. By giving these dwarf mice injections of nucleic acids, I was able to extend their life expectancy more than 200 per cent. Their specific aging patterns were definitely slowed down. The experiment is still in process.

About a year ago, back in Germany, we used nucleic acids on my mother. She had fallen and sustained a complicated fracture of the pelvis bone. Doctors had to cut her open and screw things together with metal plates. After laying still for three months she made her first walking attempts and X rays showed that she was bending the metal plates and that the healing process was not fast enough. She then received nucleic acid shots to accelerate the healing process. A few weeks later we were able to relax; the fracture had healed nicely.

Dr. Benjamin Frank has done some pioneering work in this country with oral doses of RNA and DNA and deserves full credit for this interesting work. We will soon be able to read another book by Dr. Frank on nucleic acid therapy. He has also contributed to Chapter 20 here, and discussed some of his results. But now more about his previous work:

Many diseases have their origin in some kind of cellular disorder or damage. Diseased cells (and aging, if we care to call it a disease) can often be cured by supplying the cells with an abundance of their basic building materials in pure form. For instance, the idea of the "Nucleic Acid Treatment" is to supply cells with perfect, undamaged nucleic acids. As you remember, nucleic acids are the basic building blocks of DNA and RNA. The nucleic acids are isolated from young, healthy embryonic animal or plant cells.

Step by step, this is how rejuvenation occurs: Large quantities of pure RNA and DNA are taken in our diet. The undamaged nucleic acids of the RNA and DNA from our diet are incorporated into our own RNA and DNA. This probably happens when cells divide and new DNA's and RNA's are formed. The replacement of "old" nucleic acids with "young" nucleic acids represents an overall improvement or repair of our DNA and RNA. Since DNA and RNA are the key molecules for the efficient performance of the cells (and the entire body), an overall improvement of ALL cell processes should be observed—and was observed by B. Frank, M.D., who treated many patients with nucleic acids.

Dr. Frank has developed many formulations for nucleic acid treatments. These formulations contain from 300 mg to several grams of RNA and DNA and are taken daily along with a multi-vitamin, and a vitamin B complex two to three times per week. These doses were given to patients for several weeks, smaller concentrations over a long period and larger concentrations over a shorter period. Remarkable improvements were obtained, ranging from an increase in mental alertness and physical performance to a decrease in wrinkles (89, 90).

Two dogs, aged 14 and 16 years, which were close to dying from old age, were treated with nucleic acids, and recovered. One dog died in a car accident at the age of 20 and the other lived to be 23 years old. Dr. Frank's book on nucleic acid therapy is included in my list of reading (89). Nucleic acids are already on the market and can be purchased in health food stores.

It is necessary to drink large quantities of liquids whenever nucleic acids are taken orally in order to prevent the metabolites of the nucleic acids from doing damage.

Let's talk money again.

There are several methods and ways of undergoing cell therapy. The least expensive one is to use dried cell preparations and receive treatment from a doctor as an outpatient, and the most expensive is to spend at least a full week in a clinic or "sanatorium" in one of the most beautiful areas in England or Germany. In most cases you can take the ribonucleic acid treatment as an outpatient. Now let's see how much it costs and what you get for your money.

1) Cell therapy with dried cell preparations performed on outpatients costs approximately $100 to $200, including the doctors fees and examinations. Figure an extra $100 if you spend about three days in a clinic where cell therapy is administered. The prices vary a little because the cells from different organs are more or less expensive.

2) The treatment with freshly prepared cells, including a three-day stay in the clinic where the treatment is given, costs between $500 and $700. A urine examination, developed especially for cell therapy by Professor Abderhalden, is available for more complicated treatments and costs only a few dollars more.

If you want to go all the way, you can spend a full seven restful days in a "sanatorium" where you will get the most luxurious treatment under the strictest medical supervision. The cost is about $1500 to $1700. You can even bring your husband, wife or friend along for an extra $160 per week, everything included. Remember, this is not a hospital; these sanatoriums are often fancier than the highest-priced luxury hotels.

3) The price of the ribonucleic acid shots varies because it is affected by the method of isolation and the availability of the organs. The minimum number of shots is approximately six, but let's figure the prices on 12 shots because the price difference is small and because the effectiveness increases with the number of shots. Twelve shots of the geriatric, nucleic acids from 13 organs containing formulation cost approximately $70. Twelve shots of the most expensive nucleic acids cost about $220. The shots are given two at a time every second day. Any doctor can give you the shots and will charge you about $4 per visit

(isn't that quite a difference from the $15 charge we are so used to?).

When taking cell shots or nucleic acid shots you should take it easy; rest a lot, don't drink and don't smoke for best results. Cell shots and nucleic acid injections are definitely good methods to slow down the aging process, but they will not make you younger again. However, they might re-vitalize you a bit.

CHAPTER 12

"Super Cooling" and "Deep Freezing" or "Longer Life Through Lower Temperatures"

Is a gigantic deep freeze the cemetery of the future?

Super-cooling and deep-freezing are actually two completely different approaches to the aging problem, but they are often mistaken for each other. Since very little information is available for either area of research that would justify a lengthy discussion, I will briefly discuss what the general reader should know.

"Deep-freezing" deals with the possibility of having a person who had just died or is about to die of incurable illness frozen at a low temperature (minus 320 degrees Fahrenheit or lower) and stored at this low temperature until a cure for his disease has been discovered. Such hopeful thinking! The trouble with this approach is that there is no evidence that it might work. Yet, there are already more than ten deep-frozen bodies in this country awaiting revival and eternal youth.

Is it feasible? Can it work? What do the experts in this field think about it? "This madness of freezing bodies for eventual resurrection is not rational. It is hokum, and its sole purpose is to make profit from the desperate people who buy it," said Professor Theodore Malinin in an interview published in a national newspaper (93). Who is Dr. Malinin? He is a leading expert in the field of cryobiology, a professor of surgery and pathology at the University of Miami; also he is the founder of the Society for Cryobiology and editor of the Journal of Cryobiology and other journals.

But do people listen? The deep-freezing business is already well established. For instance, one can already buy an insurance policy to make sure that there is a place for him among the "cryonics," the frozen. The cost of a modern coffin, a stainless steel freezer, is approximately $6,000 and the maintenance of it will run from $600 to $800 per year. I have no doubt that the cryotorium will be the cemetery of the future. Even though we know that it is absolute nonsense and "playing" with human emotions to let ourselves be frozen in the research stage, the idea appeals to us because it keeps our hopes alive and doesn't make dying such an irrevocable final step. It is in a way a continuation of "The Great Adventure of Life and Death."

If you believe that this method of deep-freezing is at all feasible, please take a more realistic look at it. Your doctor tells you that you are suffering from an incurable disease. After the first shock you start eliminating all the different possibilities and maybe you even do some reading and research and convince yourself of the incurability of your illness. Your doctor also tells you that, if research maintains its progress in this area, it will take no more than five or six years to find a cure; but this is about five years past your deadline and you might consider signing a contract with a low temperature storage company for human bodies. You decide to see a freezer salesman. After handing you a handful of colorful brochures, he explains that for a certain fee per year your body temperature will be lowered far below the freezing point to a temperature where all biochemical reactions are brought to a standstill. You will be stored as a supercooled icicle until some time in the future when a cure for your disease is discovered. At this time they will remove you from your cold-storage space and deliver you to a hospital where you will be unthawed with the most advanced equipment and a team of doctors will cure you immediately of your disease. Once healthy again, you will continue your life as if you had just returned from a long vacation and might even have a welcome-home party similar to the going-away party you gave before you went into the freezer.

However, some questions should cross our mind. What happens if the company goes out of business before your time is up? What happens if you have paid for only five years and after five years no cure has been found? Will they have the right to throw you in the garbage? Or maybe before you were frozen you signed a blank credit card which guaranteed you unlimited mileage. What if American Express cancels your card? Since you are not really dead when you are in the freezer, can you execute your rights as a citizen such as voting, protesting or becoming a conscientious objector? Now here's a good one: What if you were drafted? Could you obtain from a doctor a statement that you are incurably ill, and then have yourself frozen? What would the government do, unfreeze you to confirm your illness? But then what if, for some biological reasons, your body could be frozen only once?

I'm not being very scientific in this chapter, since it is too early to discuss this topic adequately and seriously. There is simply too little information or research available on deep-freezing. Single cells have been frozen to very low temperatures; and when unthawed they have continued to live and divide as before.

Human sperm has also been frozen and kept at liquid nitrogen temperature for about a month. When unthawed, the sperm was used for artificial insemination and produced normal human babies. Some other experiments show encouraging results; but when researchers tried working with even very small warmblooded animals, they were not able to show any promising results. The only positively proven aspect is that it is possible to use the deep-freeze method extensively for the storage of whole organs in order to have them available when a transplant is necessary.

As I said before, all of this is very interesting and fascinating research, but even the leading researchers in this field believe that as of this date there is very little chance of successfully freezing and unfreezing a human body. The problem is that a large percentage of the body is composed of water. When the water freezes, it destroys cells and leaves nothing but a conglomerate of dead cells which are kept from decomposition by the low temperature. The first step is that chemicals must be developed that will protect cells from being destroyed by such low temperatures. Dimethylsulfoxide is one chemical that is helpful in preserving life at lower temperatures, but it surely is not what we would need to freeze a whole human body. There is some hope that some day researchers will find the needed chemicals. Just recently D. G. Whittingham of the University of Cambridge froze mice embryos at 79 degrees centigrade, kept them there for 30 minutes, and unthawed them again. Out of 186 eight-cell ova, 139 normal embryos were removed, out of which 96 developed normally after two days. The medium was quite complex, containing polyvinylpyrrolidine as the "antifreeze" agent (49). In some experiments the temperature of test animals (mice and dogs) was lowered to about 32 degrees Fahrenheit, and they survived short periods of time at this temperature. But as soon as the temperature was lowered to the point where the water in the cells froze, the animals died and could not be revived.

125

In surgery, a process called "super cooling" is used to perform operations at temperatures slightly lower than our body temperature. At this lower temperature our metabolic processes are slowed down, and this makes an operation a little easier for the surgeon. Also, some variations of the "super cooling" method have a slightly better chance of contributing to the lengthening of our life span. For instance, since metabolic processes are slowed down when the body temperature is lowered, we age at a slower rate. Naturally this topic is of great interest to the space industry where journeys to other planets might take decades or even centuries. The super cooling methods look promising but is only feasible for humans if they are in a state of absolute rest. Since we spend nearly one-half of our life sleeping, this approach might be of some value to us.

Some day we'll probably have a part-time hibernation. When we are ready for rest, we might first take a pill that will prepare our systems for the coming hours of slowed-down metabolic processes. We would then climb into a bed which is in some way sealed off, a tent of some kind. When we fall asleep the temperature would be lowered and we might inhale a gas mixture other than air. In the morning an alarm system will bring us gradually back to our normal temperature and wake us up.

An interesting point is that this method could complement the metabolic products theory discussed briefly in Chapter 7. According to this theory, aging is due to an excess of metabolic products which are not removed from the system fast enough and therefore put extreme stress on cells, interfering with the normal metabolic processes. At a lower temperature these excess metabolic products would be removed more easily and new ones would be formed at a much slower rate.

People who sleep in a relatively cool room wake up better rested than people who sleep in an overheated room. When we are tired and go to rest at night, it will take our body a certain time to recuperate and to come to an equilibrium; the time it takes to achieve this equilibrium is obviously shortened dramatically by lower temperatures. We can also speed up and help the removal of oxidation products from our system by drinking one or two glasses of water right before going to sleep. It's like flushing out our system. But don't overdo it; too much water will upset the salt balance in body fluids.

Trying to lower our body temperature during a regular work day is, however, a much more difficult problem. Almost all our biochemical reactions are catalyzed by enzymes. Enzymes are biological catalysts that control the speed of reactions without being changed themselves. Two examples are the hydrolysis of proteins into amino acids which is controlled by the enzyme protease, and the hydrolysis of lipids into glycerol and fatty acids which is controlled by an enzyme called lipase. There are literally hundreds of different enzymes, since every enzyme is concerned with one specific process only. These enzymes have different preformance curves at different temperatures, which means that if we lower the temperature ½ degree, some enzymes will be slowed down much more than others. But since every process is in some way connected with another following it or similar to it, the whole system would "go wild" in a very short time; that is, some materials would accumulate in high concentrations while others would be completely depleted due to the different rates of metabolic reactions. Summary: to prevent or slow down atherosclerosis you should exercise and concentrate on supernutrition.

CHAPTER 13

A Solution to the Atherosclerosis Problem

*This year about one million Americans will die
from cardiovascular disease.
Hardening of the arteries leads to heart disease,
senility, impotence.
The major causes of atherosclerosis can be controlled.*

In the early days of medicine the first conclusions
about biochemical processes in the human body were
drawn by examining metabolic products that the
body excreted. It was then noticed that cholesterol
was always present in varying amounts. Examination
of a large cross-section of foods showed that cholesterol was present in animal fats, meats, eggs, liver and
many other things. An average diet contains approximately 0.3 to 0.5 grams of cholesterol daily. Cholesterol is needed by your body as a precursor for vitamin D, and the sex and adrenocortical hormones and
your body also makes approximately one to two
grams of cholesterol itself every day.

The cholesterol "hysteria" was started when a study
claimed that hardening of the arteries, cholesterol deposits and serum cholesterol were connected with each
other. Since disorders such as heart disease, senility and impotence were the result of the hardening of arteries, millions of people started to remove
foods containing cholesterol from their diets. But the
results of these restrictions proved negative. There
were people who ate foods containing high quantities

of cholesterol and showed no signs of heart trouble, yet there were people who completely eliminated cholesterol from their diets and died from heart attacks.

Dr. P. D. White, the late President Eisenhower's cardiologist, sums up the confusion about cholesterol: "I must admit I'm thoroughly confused about cholesterol and, for that matter, I'm not sure whether some of the weight control diets might not be dangerous to the heart." And Dr. J. D. Wassersug says: "It is almost impossible to regulate the amount of cholesterol in the blood by manipulating the diet." (114, 115).

But the question to ask is: Why doesn't the cholesterol ingested from foods affect the serum cholesterol level in a healthy person? It is simply because the body has what the biochemist calls a "feedback mechanism." That is, when you take in more cholesterol than you need, your body stops making it.

Hardening of the arteries, called arteriosclerosis, is caused by cholesterol deposits *and* the presence of triglycerides (fats). It was long believed that the hardening of arteries was caused by the "typical American diet" (which is high in cholesterol, fats and carbohydrates). Recently this idea received strong support from Professor R. Wissler of the University of Chicago (50). He reported that Rhesus monkeys, when fed a "typical American" diet for two years, developed four times as many arteriosclerotic deposits than monkeys fed a diet low in fats, refined sugar and cholesterol. This evidence is very valuable because the metabolism of rhesus monkeys is very similar to the human metabolism.

However, in order to prevent arteriosclerosis, you have to control the level of triglycerides (fats) in your blood. Triglycerides are fats (discussed in Chapter 4). The amount of fats you ingest is determined by the type of food you eat (53) and this in turn determines the triglyceride level in the blood stream. If you study a good book on nutrition you will know which foods are high in fats and carbohydrates. So, if you want to control the amounts of fats in your blood, you must watch your diet carefully. Although fat diets are relatively inexpensive and high protein diets are expensive, the difference in cost can lick the fat problem.

Recent research results will convince you that it is possible to prevent hardening of the arteries and high levels of cholesterol deposits. Professor Mumma of the Pennsylvania State University reported that a compound made with vitamin C might be able to prevent or even reverse hardening of the arteries. He discovered that ascorbic acid (vitamin C) alone doubled the cholesterol excretion in test animals. Creating a vitamin C derivative, he then fed it to test animals and increased their cholesterol excretion 50 times over the normal rate (51). In England Dr. C. Spittle has shown that vitamin C therapy can control cholesterol deposits and remove deposits that are already present (116). In Russia, where the medical profession does not try so hysterically to refute the value of vitamin C, scientists have long recognized the value of vitamin C and prescribe it almost always for patients with arteriosclerosis.

Another favorable report comes from Professor Grossman of Chicago University. He experimented with another natural product (an acid mucopolysaccharide) and was able to control cholesterol deposits in test animals.

Lecithin can remove cholesterol deposits due to its detergent-like characteristics (94). Lecithin has also been shown to play an important role in keeping the blood system in good order; it is an inexpensive compound which is available in drug and health food stores.

But this is not the whole story. Vitamins B, E and A also have been shown to play an important role in controlling cholesterol. Dr. L. B. Dotti and his co-workers at St. Luke's Hospital in New York have fed rabbits cholesterol and inositol and demonstrated that these animals had a 181% cholesterol increase compared to a 337% increase in rabbits which did not get inositol (117). Nicotinic acid (vitamin B_3) has also been shown to control cholesterol levels (118). Some side effects of nicotinic acid, such as flushing of the skin, disappeared when a derivative of nicotinic acid, niacin amide, was used (118). Rats with hyper-cholesterolemia were studied to show the effect of vitamin A on the cholesterol level. R. Amer and P. Lachance demonstrated that the cholesterol levels decreased as the vitamin A activity was increased (119).

About 600,000 Americans will die this year from heart attacks. By simply providing yourself with the proper vitamins and lecithin you can protect yourself to a large extent from this disease. Other risk factors of coronary disease are hypertension, diabetes mellitus, smoking and physical inactivity (53).

Why smoking again? Toxic materials that you inhale pass through the lungs right into the blood stream. These materials will attack the walls of the arteries first. If free radicals are formed, vitamin E in the blood can deactivate them and thus prevent damage to the arteries. When you smoke a cigarette, the inhaled nicotine stimulates your body to release adrenalin. The released adrenalin again causes fat cells in your body to release "fat components" into your blood stream. Here you have one of the reasons why "cigarette smoking may be hazardous to your health:" an increased triglyceride level.

Several studies have shown that amounts of physical activity also control cholesterol deposits. The

Irish-Boston heart study demonstrated this point quite clearly when it showed that people on high cholesterol diets developed fewer heart problems when they were active and exercised.

Physical activity burns up cholesterol and also prevents it from being deposited. However, cholesterol might still be harmful for persons whose normal regulating mechanisms are impaired and who have certain diseases, such as hyperlipoproteinemia.

There are about 15 groups of drugs that can help prevent arteriosclerosis; they either affect cholesterol absorption or synthesis, or help to control the triglyceride level in your flood (53). But some anticholesterol drugs were given to hundreds of thousands of people before the government removed this drug from the market because it caused the loss of hair, loss of sexual desire, blindness and other ill effects. But why take a chance with drugs? I think that we should prefer to use the natural compounds such as vitamins.

There are some good research results available that suggest that carbohydrates are even more dangerous than fats (115, 120). But we discussed the dangers of carbohydrates in Chapter 4.

Ask yourselves, "Why is the drug industry so interested in getting new drugs registered?" Is it just for the sake of being able to sell another drug? Why are doctors so reluctant in prescribing natural compounds that researchers have shown to be effective? I believe that you should try to do everything right WITHOUT the use of drugs. Compounds such as vitamins and other materials with which the body is already familiar cannot be classified as drugs.

In the light of all these findings, you definitely should re-evaluate your nutritional habits before you eliminate valuable nutrients like eggs and milk from your diets. I eat at least three eggs per day and I know of many others who do the same; and we certainly don't have any heart problems or increased cholesterol levels.

There was a time when men outnumbered women in the incidence of death from heart attack by a ratio of 12 to 1; but times have changed. Dr. D. Spain of Brookdale Hospital Medical Center found that the ratio has changed to 4 to 1 and he has enough evidence to show that this decreased ratio is due to an increased cigarette consumption among women (108).

If atherosclerosis, cholesterol and heart disease are of special interest to you, you should read the remarkably clarifying paper by Dr. Passwater (115).

A. M. Nelson, M.D., reported a study on 206 patients with coronary artery disease in *Geriatrics* of December 1972 and came to the conclusion that a fat-controlled diet high in protein and in seafoods (except shellfish) can benefit patients beyond the age of 55 (134).

I believe this diet deserves some special attention; I therefore quote:

The dietary plan is formulated around the basic food groups essential to good health. This dietary method enables the patient to have food variety while he is simultaneously obtaining the requisite body nutrients. A meal plan for any single day would include selections from the following food categories:

1. Milk or milk products. One pint or more of non-fat milk or buttermilk is recommended. Low-fat cottage cheese and certain low-fat cheeses also are allowed.

2. Meat, poultry or fish. A total daily allowance of 6 oz. of cooked lean beef, lamb, veal, chicken or turkey is permitted. The patient is encouraged to substitute seafood for meat, in unlimited amounts, at least three

times a week. Lean pork or ham and shellfish may each be served once a week as a substitute for the meat in the diet.

3. Vegetables and fruits. The patient should have dark green or yellow vegetables, tomatoes, or citrus fruits at least four times a day.

4. Bread and cereals. The patient should eat four or more servings of enriched or whole grain products daily.

5. Unsaturated fats. A daily intake of three tablespoons of fat, including that used for cooking, is the maximum amount permitted in this diet. Safflower and corn oils, corn oil and safflower mayonnaise, or safflower and corn oil margarine may be used.

CHAPTER 14

Modern Vampires, the Blood Rejuvenators

Do you remember seeing one of those monster movies where the vampire sneaked into the bedroom of the pretty young girl and, after sucking her blood, was able to live forever? Well, we would do it a little differently but recent research results suggest that receiving blood from a young person, giving blood or having your blood cleansed with modern equipment could extend your life expectancy tremendously.

But before we talk about these new methods which are already being practiced, let's talk a little about blood, its functions and what it contains, so that we can understand the reasoning behind these new methods a little better.

Blood has many different functions. It carries oxygen and foods to the cells and carbon dioxide and oxidation products from the cells. Besides this it carries blood cells, antibodies, hormones, enzymes and minerals. How can it do all those things at one time? Let's analyze a sample of blood. We have about five to six quarts of blood in our body. It consists of two parts: a liquid called plasma and suspended particles in the blood—the red blood cells, white blood cells and platelets.

The red blood cells contain iron in the center of a large molecule called hemoglobin and transport the oxygen. This is a very sensitive molecule and is easily destroyed when it comes in contact with toxic materials like carbon monoxide, for example. Carbon monoxide is contained in automobile exhaust fumes and in cigarette smoke.

The white blood cells (the leukocytes) are a major part of the defensive mechanism of our body; they destroy invading microorganisms and serve as a protection against infections. Some of the different white blood cells are lymphocytes, basophils, monocytes and neutrophils, and a white blood count, when above normal, indicates an infection. A large number of white blood cells are found in the lungs because here the chance is very high that bacteria and other foreign matter may enter our system. Comparison of the corroded lungs of a smoker with the lungs of a nonsmoker clearly demonstrates the lower resistance of cigarette smokers to diseases.

The platelets play an important role in the clotting of blood.

The liquid phase in which the solid particles are suspended, the plasma, contains about 92% water. About seven to eight percent consists of blood proteins which are mainly albumins, globulins and fibrinogen.

Fibrinogen plays an important role in blood clotting, together with other components of the blood.

The albumins are mainly responsible for maintaining a constant osmotic pressure. Osmosis is a complex process which takes place in plants and animals, and the overall result is the control of the water balance in the entire system.

The globulins are the most important group of blood proteins. The number of these different proteins is quite large but there are two main groups. One group consists of proteins that form complex compounds with foodstuffs in order to transport it throughout the body. The other group of proteins consists of valuable antibodies which give us immunity against numerous diseases.

We know a lot about blood proteins but the area is not yet well researched. We know especially little about certain proteins which are found only in very small quantities. Besides the compounds described above, there are about 50 other compounds in the blood including hormones, enzymes and minerals.

Since water is a very good heat conductor and since the blood circulates through all parts of the body it serves another very important purpose which is to keep the temperature of the body constant. This is especially important because the enzyme activity changes dramatically with a change in temperature. Remember, enzymes are compounds that control chemical reactions. This is one major reason why it would be extremely difficult to lengthen our life span by lowering our body temperature. Bottlenecks of chemicals would build up and upset the chemistry of the entire system. However, it is possible that especially long-lived people have a body which is slightly lower in temperature than that of the average person. But if such a temperature difference really exists, it was not created artifically. I am well aware of the research results obtained by Dr. R. D. Myers at Purdue University, who was able to lower or raise the temperature of animals by injecting them with certain specific ions. We might use this in the future to increase body temperature, for example, to help our own body fight an infection, or to lower it to slow down the metabolism during an operation.

Waste materials are removed by the filtration action of the kidneys. The functions of the kidney are actually very simple to understand. Relatively wide blood vessels enter and exit from the kidneys. Inside the kidneys the blood vessels form fine capillaries which are in contact with another capillary system which drains into the bladder. At first almost all dissolved materials are filtered out, but then the important compounds are selectively reabsorbed.

Some diseases of the blood are:

Anemia: an abnormally low red blood count.

Polycythemia: an abnormally high red blood count.

Leukopenia: when there is a dramatic decrease in the number of leukocytes.

Leukemia: when there is an overproduction of leukocytes.

Hemophilia: when the absence of certain chemicals prevents the blood from clotting.

The acidity of the blood is kept constant by three different buffer systems. This again is extremely important for the normal functioning of our body. Whenever you drink too much water you wash out many important minerals necessary for these and other processes. That can happen, for example, if you are on the Number One diet idiocy, namely proteins and lots of water only.

After this introduction on the functions of blood we can take a look at the exciting experiments performed by Professor F. C. Ludwig at the University of California which were reported in the transactions of the New York Academy of Sciences in November 1972. In one of the major experiments Professor Ludwig put two rats, a young animal and an old one, in some kind of contraption where they could move around a little, and joined their blood systems. The process is called parabiosis and allows a constant exchange of blood between the old and the young animal. The old animals in these experiments by far outlived the controls, that is the animals that were not hooked up to another animal. These results are remarkable, especially since the hooked-up animals were under a special kind of stress. How can we explain these extraordinary results? No exact answer to this question is possible. We have several possibilities:

1) The resistance of the older animals to diseases could have been increased and so their life span was increased.

2) As described earlier, older cells produce enzymes and other materials that are less effective than the ones produced by young cells. Fresh cell therapy, as practiced by the followers of Professor Niehans, uses cell materials from embryonic cells in order to supply older cells with the rejuvenating powers of young cells. These results actually fit very nicely into Dr. Niehans' theory on aging. Yet, what actually causes the rejuvenation is not known.

3) It is also possible that the blood contains what some people call aging factors. What these aging factors are and how they work can only be guessed. In part accordance with the oxidation product theory on aging, it is also possible that certain oxidation products accumulate in our system and cause aging. By connecting an old animal to the blood system of a younger one we simply could have diluted these aging factors or they could have been excreted by the excretory system of the younger, better-functioning animal.

Other research results by D. Bodenstein at the Research Center of Gerontology in Baltimore suggest that the young animals supplied the old ones with some special youth factors. Dr. Bodenstein joined cockroaches in parabiosis and found that the old animal was able to regenerate limbs, a characteristic which is normally only found in young animals. What does that mean to us? It means that some day we might be able to lengthen our life span by having blood transfusions from a young person. Blood transfusions are everyday procedures in hospitals and take only a few minutes. The cost would be approximately $60 per pint. But before you start looking for a young blood donor, let me tell you about another interesting area of research.

Based on the idea that, as you get older, aging factors appear in your blood that cause the aging of the entire body, some interesting research is going on at the Orentreich Medical Foundation in New York. What if we could remove these aging factors from our blood? Then we should be able to delay aging, shouldn't we? But how can we remove these aging factors from the blood? Simple. With the help of a process called plasmapherisis. In this process blood is withdrawn, centrifuged, and then the blood cells are returned to the body without the plasma which contains the aging factors. Within the next few months several results on different test animals will be available from the Orentreich Foundation which will hopefully show us the degree of life prolongation that can result from plasmapherisis. I talked to Dr. Orentreich and he informed me that results obtained so far on test animals show that plasmapheresis has a favorable effect on the cholesterol metabolism and that it slows down cross-linking in collagen. These results and the plasmapherisis results obtained from humans are sufficiently promising for us to go full steam ahead with this line of research.

But how much does such a process cost, and how safe is it? Well, if you are a healthy specimen, you can actually get money for having this plasmapherisis done on you, believe it or not. How come? Simply because hospitals need plasma. Plasma is a valuable fluid which is needed for transfusions and blood banks are paying good money for it. Plasmapherisis can be done twice a week and the protein content of your blood is back to normal within eight hours if you eat right.

Plasmapherisis takes about one hour and it is done while you sit in a comfortable armchair and read your favorite magazine. Naturally you get a medical examination at first and then a needle is inserted in your arm and one pint of blood is removed—it's just like giving blood. The blood is then centrifuged and the blood cells are returned into your blood system with a physiological solution. The whole process is then repeated once more and somebody gives you between $10 and $15. Everything is done through one needle. After having plasmapherisis done four times you have replaced about 50% of your original total blood volume.

If removing aging factors from the blood can lengthen your life span, then giving blood should have the same life-extending effect. The only trouble is that you cannot give blood as often as you can have plasmapherisis. What can you loose? You always wanted to be a good guy and give blood anyway.

I have had plasmapherisis done on me several times already and I haven't been able to observe any negative side effects.

Our hospitals often have a serious blood shortage. This is due to people being afraid to give blood and also to an antiquated blood donor system. There is absolutely no reason to be afraid because giving blood or plasma is a simple, fast and painless procedure. Most hospitals rely on voluntary blood donors and it is often looked down on for a person to sell his blood. For these reasons we have a constant blood shortage and often have to take blood from wherever we can get it. This often includes blood from skid row characters and other unhealthy specimens. In Europe it is a common thing to take money for your blood because most insurances cover the cost of blood transfusions. Many European students have furnished themselves with extra spending money by giving blood. This is actually encouraged and therefore there are enough donors and blood banks can be selective. Skid row characters, drunks and people with an unhealthy appearance don't even make it past the doors.

I believe we should strongly encourage giving blood for money, especially among healthy younger people. But perhaps the possibility of extending life through giving blood or plasma will help this situation.

CHAPTER 15

Youth Drugs

*"Control of aging is synonymous with extension
of life. If you have 100,000 men age 20, about
100 of them will die from all causes in any one
year. If you have 100,000 men age 80, about
20,000 of them will die in any one year. So the
survival percentage, by age, is impressive. Yet,
if the physiology of an 80-year-old could be
kept on the same level as a 20-year-old, the
probability of death in any one year would
drop enormously."*

Johan Bjorksten

Just a few years ago youth drugs would have been
classified strictly as a matter for science fiction, but
now they have become a reality. Scientists around the
world are already testing the efficiency of youth
drugs, and the research results look terrific (55). The
diligent work of the researchers in many countries has
already contributed to solving part of the problem.
Researchers have come to the point where they have
identified many aspects of the problem and are now
systematically arranging the pieces of information to
fit the whole picture. There are many methods of attacking the problem, but the two most important are
the prevention of aging effects and the undoing of already existing aging damage. Furthermore, both
methods should be performed with chemicals which
the body is already familiar with, such as components
of nutrients or specific enzymes.

But before I discuss these methods, first take a look

143

at the different ways in which scientists are trying to lengthen or improve life.

In Chapter 6 we have learned that the body can react towards compounds that are formed during aging by starting immunological reactions, and we also know that the body reacts towards foreign matter which is not characteristic to the body by starting immunologic reactions. It is as if the body recognizes an enemy and starts to alert its defenses. The problem is that larger molecules or damaged molecules, which are formed in the aging process, are often identified by the body as foreign matter, which starts off the immunologic reactions and the body literally attacks itself. Naturally, an aged and slightly confused immunologic system could show the same response.

R. Walford used an immunosuppressive chemical (azathioprine) to check if a decreased immunologic reaction could prolong the life span of test animals. When he tested the drug on mice, he found that he was able to extend their survival rate by approximately 50% (56).

D. Bellamy tested another drug, prednisolone, and obtained fantastic results with mice as his test animals. For example, survival was about 10% without prednisolone while it was about 85% with prednisolone (57).

Another sign of aging is the accumulation of lipofuscin deposits in the cells, especially in brain cells. Researchers believe that the accumulation of lipofuscin has something to do with a decrease in our mental performance in old age. A drug called meclofenoxate, which was studied by K. Nandy and G. Bourne, reduced lipofuscin deposits in guinea pigs (58). Other drugs like magnesium orotate and kawain can also control lipofuscin deposits (59, 60). Also, learning ability and memory are closely connected with protein synthesis in the brain cells. Chemicals are now being tested which are thought to increase or to bring back to normal the protein synthesis that is connected with learning and memory functions (63, 64, 65).

Professor R. Williams found that pantothenic acid can increase the average life span of mice. A number of mice were divided into two groups and received a standard diet. The only difference between the two groups was that one group received an extra 0.3 milligram of pantothenic acid. The average life span was 550 days for the group without pantothenic acid and 653 days for the group that received the pantothenic acid (69). The reason why pantothenic acid has such a remarkable effect is probably as follows: a compound called coenzyme-A is an extremely important compound in our metabolic pathways. Our body can make this coenzyme A from pantothenic acid and other compounds.

Procaine, H-3, KH-3: Procaine was synthesized in 1905 by Einhorn and was initially used as an anesthetic. Later the drug received attention because it was studied by the Romanian Professor Aslan as a geriatric drug. Professor Aslan observed that older people, when treated with procaine for several months, demonstrated remarkable rejuvenating effects. The application of procaine was administered in the form of injections which made the long-term treatment somewhat difficult. An oral formula of procaine was subsequently developed by a German company (126). This oral formula contains procaine hydrochloride and haematoporphyrin. Several researchers worked with this drug and reported good results (127, 128, 129, 130).

Studies by Ting and Coon have demonstrated what happens to procaine in our body. It is hydrolized to give p-aminobenzoic acid and diethylaminoethanol. P-aminobenzoic acid is part of the vitamin B complex and is also an enzyme-buildingstone. Diethylaminoethanol is known in medicine as a blood-pressure-regulating substance.

The haematoporphyrin has a regulating effect on our nervous system and is also known as a drug for treating psychic depressions. In addition haematoporphyrin acts on the gonads and can therefore increase the functions of the testes and ovaries.

The KH-3 formulation is not yet sold in the USA since the FDA has doubts about the value and effects of this drug. However, long-term animal tests have been performed which showed that the animals which were treated with KH-3 demonstrated over-all improved health without any side effects. Tests performed on patients in Germany also showed the absence of any negative side effects.

Now KH-3 has a registration number with the FDA and hopefully you will be able to buy it in the USA soon. It certainly is no "wonder drug" that makes raving sex maniacs out of old men and women. In Germany I talked to a representative of Schwarzhaupt Company and was told of many good results that were obtained with KH-3, but when I asked the company for a statement in writing that summarized these facts I didn't hear from them again. This silence surprised me and at first I thought there must be some bad side effects connected with this drug, but some intensive research that included experimental results disclosed at the twenty-fifth Annual Meeting of the Gerontological Society in December 1972 convinced me that this was not the case. The most likely explanation I could come up with was that the Schwarzhaupt people didn't want to upset the FDA with any statement about their drug that might appear in an American book.

The most recent research results concerning procaine hydrochloride are as follows: Robinson and co-workers demonstrated a strong connection between relatively high levels of monoamine oxidase in the serum and brain with the aging process (131). Other researchers, Hrachovec et al., at the University of Southern California, demonstrated that procaine hydrochloride is a monoamine oxidase inhibitor (132). J. P. Hrachovec disclosed at the December 1972 meeting of the Gerontological Society that procaine hydrochloride also inhibits monoamine oxidase in the liver of test animals (133).

These findings suggest that procaine hydrochloride could be even more beneficial when taken at an earlier age. We know that aging is a continuous process which starts very early in life. If the aging process of nondividing cells like brain cells could be slowed down at an early stage of life, we should be able to see some dramatic results. But again, it will take some time to prove it.

S. and C. Friedman administered pituitary hormones to rats which were 24 months old. The mortality rate during the following month decreased dramatically (61, 62).

Dr. Bjorksten, at the Bjorksten Research Laboratory in Madison, Wisconsin, takes a more basic approach in solving the aging problem. Dr. Bjorksten works with enzymes and tries to undo the damage which has already been done by the aging process; his goal is to reverse the effects of cross-link damage. Success in this area would mean a reversal of the aging process. The excellent results that Dr. Bjorksten has already achieved were already discussed in Chapter 6. In fact, I recently talked with Dr. Bjorksten and he is extremely optimistic about the progress of his research (84, 68).

It is not necessary to mention cell therapy and nucleic acids again because these areas have already been covered in Chapter 11 as have been my own results with nucleic acids.

Another step towards the attainment of eternal

youth has been taken by R. Passwater, a consultant in gerontology at American Gerontological Laboratories Inc. There, many age-retarding drug formulations have been tested already, and the first Investigative New Drug applications (IND) were filed with the FDA in 1970. Dr. Passwater strongly believes in the "Free Radical" theory and also concentrates heavily on radiation protection and protein missynthesis (discussed in Chapters 5 and 6). According to Dr. Passwater, protection from radicals should increase our life span by five to ten years; protection from radiation adds another two to five years; and prevention of protein missynthesis should give an additional five to ten years. Since all three are believed to act synergistically (working together), the total life span increase could be 30 to 40 years (17). These estimates were made in early 1971 and more recent results clearly indicate even greater rates of longevity.

The chemicals tested at the American Gerontologic Laboratories Inc. are combinations of antioxidants, such as sulfur amino acids (cysteine, cystine, methionine), vitamin E (very important), selenium compounds, and other antioxidants (1,70). It should be pointed out here that it would be extremely dangerous for anyone to experiment on himself with selenium compounds since they are extremely toxic. Selenium compounds must be taken in exact quantities together with other compounds which, in turn, decrease their toxic effects and raise the tolerance level.

The latest results have shown that it was possible to extend the average life span of mice 166% by using combinations of vitamin E, cystein, selenium compounds and other antioxidants together with an excellent diet (71). Many researchers have obtained good results from their experimentation with antioxidants, but no one got even close to 166%. Radical protection seems to be more and more important. Radicals can be quite different in reactivity and structure, which is

148

probably the reason why such good results are obtained with a mixture of different antioxidants. Each antioxidant can probably deactivate a specific type of radical. Still, there is another possible explanation for these good results with antioxidants. The Russian scientist T. Bernstein found that when the antioxidants sodium selenite and vitamin E were used together, this caused an increased formation of antibodies (155). Possibly this helped the immunologic system in its defense against incoming toxic materials.

Naturally it will be a few years before some of these drugs are on the market in the correct concentrations. In order to test the effectiveness of all new "youth drugs," a number of tests have been devised which are associated with the aging process. But we cannot simply take a group of people, feed them drugs and wait until they die. More sophisticated methods have to be devised to test the effectiveness of these drugs. Large groups of volunteers are also needed to take these drugs and to undergo regular medical check-ups at prescribed time intervals.

Alterations of the normal aging patterns can probably be detected within a five to ten year period. Many other signs associated with aging (e.g., physical fitness, wrinkling, skin tone, blood pressure and mental alertness) will probably show improvements in a shorter time (17). If other tests (for cholesterol levels, etc.) show additional improvements, the status of new drugs could be changed to the New Drug Applications stage (NDA) and further testing on a larger scale would give conclusive evidence. Three large-scale tests involving matched groups of 300 to 6000 people have already been devised. However, it will take money and time to establish the value of these test results and drugs.

But is there anything you can do in the meantime? Or do you have to wait until the FDA gives its approval? Fortunately there is a lot that can be done. The basic ingredients of these new drugs are not secret, and there are a number of available nutrients which are rich in these compounds. Some selenium-rich nutrients are herring, anchovetta, wheat germ, tuna, bran, broccoli, cabbages, onions, tomatoes and brewer's yeast. Sulfur amino acids are contained in eggs, cabbage and muscle meats in above-normal concentrations. Vitamin E is found in wheat germ oil, eggs, muscle meat, fish, whole wheat and vegetable oils. Vitamins E and C are sold in drug stores without prescription, and it appears that no damage is caused by large doses of these vitamins. Also, many protein preparations sold in health and drug stores contain high concentrations of the desired sulfur amino acids, and I am quite sure that many other products will appear on the market as soon as there is a demand for them. Nucleic acids can be obtained from fish, sea foods, nuts, brewer's yeast and caviar.

Scientists do not really know too much about the reactions of our body to large doses of vitamins. More research results are urgently needed. Therefore you should be aware of the fact that you might be taking a risk if you decide to take large quantities of vitamins. However, from the research results available so far I personally believe that the risk is very small.

Doctors often accuse Pauling of recommending too high vitamin C dosages for curing a cold (approximately six g. per day). I personally know the manager of a health club who takes approximately 20 grams (20,000 mg) every day. The man has ten children and is a typical example of a healthy specimen.

I am often asked which vitamins and compounds a person should take each day. I cannot conclusively answer this question since sufficient research results are not yet available. The requirements for the different vitamins also change from person to person. For example, we can measure the spillover level for vitamin C; that means we give a person more and more vitamin C and measure the point when the body has enough and it spills over. This spillover point can be drastically different for two persons of the same sex, age and weight. The requirements often vary and we just have to find out ourselves what and how much is good enough. But I know what some other people are taking, and I can tell you which vitamins and other compounds I am taking. Let me make it clear that I am not recommending these doses. You might take the vitamins and other compounds I am taking as a guideline; the correct amounts for yourself, however, you will have to decide yourself. Make sure that you are not allergic to any one of these compounds or that an illness or other condition might prevent you from taking them.

Now that I have made myself perfectly clear, here is what I take every day (my weight is 173 pounds):

Two balanced B-complex vitamins in which the B-1, B-2 and B-6 vitamins are in the 10 mg. range. All together there are about 10 vitamins in this formulation.

Vitamin E: 600 to 800 mg.

Vitamin A: 25,000 units

Vitamin C: 1000 to 3000 mg. I take a little more when I am under stress, and up to 9000 mg. per day if I feel a cold coming on.

Pantothenic acid: an extra 50 mg. (also in the B-complex).

Niacin amide: an extra 200 to 400 mg.

Minerals containing iodine, manganese, zinc, copper and iron (traces).

Calcium and magnesium (carbonate or bone meal) with vitamin D. Calcium and magnesium amounting to approximately 500 mg. each.

Cystein hydrochloride: (sulfur amino acid) 400 to 600 mg.

Lecithin: about 1 g.

Safflower oil: 1 to 2 teaspoons (contains essential fatty acid).

Dried liver: 5 tablets about twice a week.

Wheat germ oil: 1 to 2 teaspoons.

Brewers yeast: about 6 tablets after every meal.

I wouldn't even touch an aspirin with a ten foot pole.

I take these vitamins and other compounds spread through the day always after meals. Don't take any iron together with vitamin E.

Every three to four months I take what is called "Nucleic Acid Cure." For about three weeks I take about 1200 to 2000 mg of a nucleic acid preparation three to four times per week. After the three weeks I take only 200 mg three to four times per week. Whenever I take larger quantities of nucleic acids, I drink a lot of liquids to prevent any effects for the metabolites of nucleic acids.

I have also taken Regeneresen shots in Germany. Regeneresen are the organ-specific nucleic acids described in Chapter 11. I took the shots, even though I am still far from the age of 40, because I wanted to see if I could observe any after-effects and since I believed that there was absolutely no chance of negative side effects. I felt remarkably good after the shots, but one could attribute this to a good vacation I was having at the time. However, I felt just a little too good for a vacation, and there was something else I noticed. I am allergic to ragweed, mold and dust. When the ragweed season starts I normally suffer immediately without condeming the cause. The year I took the Regeneresen shots I felt no effects from the ragweed until about three weeks after the season had started, while friends were suffering all around me. Whether there is any connection here I really can't tell.

PART IV

Do It Now, And Die Later, Much Later

If your goal is to stay young in mind and body, and if you plan to take youth compounds that will extend your life expectancy past its present maximum, you will have to fulfill some basic requirements. These are:

1) Super nutrition
2) A moderate exercise program
3) No smoking
4) Elimination of major stress factors
5) Clean air

All five are closely connected with each other and you must try to do almost everything right in each area. Completely neglecting one or more areas will drastically decrease your chances of achieving the goal.

Warning: The Surgeon General Has Determined That Cigarette Smoking Is Dangerous To Your Health

During this year approximately 350,000 Americans will die from cancer—600,000 Americans will die from heart attack. A major cause of cancer and heart attack is cigarette smoking.

Cigarettes smoking makes you age faster.

"We determined that sputum cytology was unquestionably the most effective way to detect lung cancer and was superior to any other method and all other methods in combination."
William O. Rusell, M.D.

"We saw a forty-fold decrease in the number of carcinomas in situ in the ex-cigarette smokers when compared with individuals of the same age group who had continued to smoke."
Oscar Auerbach, M.D.

Here are the facts: This year alone about 350,000 people will die from cancer in the USA. The lung cancer death rate for smokers is 1000 (one thousand) percent higher than for nonsmokers (77). Besides cancer, smoking can also cause heart disease, emphysema and ulcers (45, 81). Cardiovascular diseases, which cause about 50% of the mortality in the USA, are attributed to smoking, cholesterol and hypertension (82). Naturally, you think you will never get cancer, especially if you are a heavy smoker. But face the facts: If you are a heavy smoker, I believe that you have a better chance of surviving a fall from a tenth floor window than of not dying from the effects of smoking.

What happens when you smoke a cigarette? You light up, the tobacco starts burning, and you inhale tar, nicotine, carbon monoxide and other poisonous gases, all of which are related, without any doubt, to the diseases mentioned above. The oxidation products of a cigarette can also generate *radicals* which can shorten your life span by increasing the rate of the aging process.

Now let's examine the mortality ratio and compare smokers with nonsmokers. Assume that we want to study the death rate caused by lung cancer among smokers and nonsmokers. We would study two large groups of people, say 10,000 in each category. Over a certain time period we record every death due to lung cancer. The mortality ratio is then figured:

$$\text{Mortality Ratio:} \quad \frac{\text{number of deaths in smoker group}}{\text{number of deaths in the nonsmoker group}}$$

If, in a certain time period, 800 died in the smoker group and only 87 in the nonsmoker group, the Mortality Ratio would be 800/87. This would mean that nearly ten times more people died of lung cancer in the smoker group than in the nonsmoker group.

Impossible, you say, the number can't be that high? Who would allow a product to be sold if it has such a high toxicity? But, in fact, the mortality ratio for lung cancer among smokers is almost exactly nine. Some other mortality ratios for smokers are: bronchitis and emphysema 2.3, esophagus 5.8, stomach ulcers 4.3 and larynx cancer 11 (83). Do you understand what these numbers mean? If you are a heavy smoker (15 to 20 cigarettes per day or more), you either have to quit or get used to the idea that you will probably die from cancer or some other disease caused by smoking.

Every cigarette you smoke is a potential cancer or heart disease hazard; every cigarette you don't smoke is a definite improvement. Naturally, the more you smoke the larger the risk; but it seems that once you smoke more than eight cigarettes per day, you are already on the losing side. Why are only a few cigarettes per day so harmful? A healthy lung needs a fine, fast vibrating movement to clean itself out. Smoking stops the vibration and as a result the lung doesn't clean itself any more, resulting in smoker's cough.

If you want a good chance to live longer, you'll have to quit smoking sooner or later. Heavy smokers normally can't stop overnight. But the best thing to do is to cut down a little at a time in order to realize just how much of a slave to the nicotine habit you actually are. I know it's hard to quit; I had to do it myself. The first important step is not to smoke the whole cigarette. Of all the nicotine and tar in a cigarette you get only about 25% of it in the first half. About 75% is in the other half since the tobacco acts like a filter and absorbs some of the nicotine and tar which is first produced. This way your body gets used to the smaller quantities of toxic materials and when you finally quit the withdrawal symptoms will not be as strong.

The biggest problem, however, if you want to quit smoking, is psychological. The second step after cutting down on the number of cigarettes smoked is to un-brainwash yourself. You have to learn all the facts about cigarette smoking so that, each time you light a cigarette, you remember that this burning piece of paper and weeds

a) Doesn't make you sexier, no matter what the cigarette advertisement is trying to insinuate— it actually decreases your sex life.
b) Doesn't improve your looks—actually to somebody who knows the facts about smoking you look pretty weak and stupid.

c) Doesn't give you a lift—it actually decreases your performance in every possible area.
d) Doesn't calm your nerves—it actually helps to destroy nerve tissue.
e) DOESN'T DO ANYTHING THAT IS GOOD FOR YOU.

But what it really does is keep you hooked and brainwashed so that you actually spend money on something that decreases your chance to live, more than anything else you inhale, or even push down your throat.

That the aging process is accelerated by smoking is also indicated by the fact that smoking helps to cause wrinkles. Dr. H. Daniell studied more than 1000 persons and found that there is a definite correlation between the formation of wrinkles, smoking time and the number of cigarettes smoked (85).

W. S. Rickert and W. F. Forbes at the University of Waterloo, Ontario, examined the effects of cigarette smoke on lung collagen and came to the following conclusion: "These results suggest that some of the collagen changes, brought about by normal aging, may be accelerated by exposure to cigarette smoke" (149). Also, if you believe that our curative methods for lung cancer are effective, you should look at a paper by Dr. H. J. Sullivan in "Geriatrics". Out of 594 lung cancer patients seen between 1966 and 1968 only 40 are still alive (156). This is the true story of bronchogenic carcinoma.

A team headed by Dr. M. Stanton from the National Cancer Institute reported another cigarette-cancer link. "It was possible to cause lung cancer in rats by exposing them to the cigarette tar product of only five cigarettes."

When you inhale that country fresh flavor, you inhale about 30 chemicals that can aide in cancer formation. Several are "complete carcinogens," that means that they can start cancer all by themselves.

Lung Cancer goes through several well-defined stages until it becomes cancer that can be detected by X-rays. Those stages are: normal—inflammatory—atypical—malignant in situ—malignant invasive. Only malignant invasive can be detected by X-rays. A new method, "sputum cytology," can detect the inflammatory state. It merely involves coughing into a plastic bottle on four consecutive mornings and returning the bottle to the examiner. This method is simple, inexpensive and of the greatest importance for early lung cancer detection.

TO QUIT SMOKING IS DEFINITELY WORTH IT. Often one gets the following argument from heavy cigarette smokers: "I have smoked for many years; if there is any damage it is already too late." WRONG. Studies of mortality ratios have shown that the chance of getting cancer decreases rapidly if you quit smoking. Dr. Oscar Auerbach, M.D., has studied this problem and reports: "We have additional evidence that when you stop painting the tracheobronchial tree with a carcinogenic agent, those cells that are progressing toward cancer shrivel away, contract, disintegrate, and disappear" (112).

Why don't you evaluate the situation?
Kick the habit!
Leave cancer country!

CHAPTER 17

Such A Deal

"The most important point in keeping active is that when one reaches, say, 65, one will be physically fit. The tragedy is not so much an early demise as it is incapacity around and beyond the retirement age."

CARLETON B. CHAPMAN

Professor of Medicine
at the University of Texas
Science American, 212,96 (1965)

The best starting points for a longer, happier life begin with good nutrition and physical fitness. Most people think that nutrition is easy to maintain and that exercise is really hard, unenjoyable work. Wrong! An important thing to remember is that you don't need to exercise for the sake of exercise alone. Choose some sports or activities that you enjoy and participate in them as often as you can. In fact, a recent study on exercise revealed that people who have a regular (light to medium) exercise program actually live longer than both "super athletes" and those who do no exercise at all.

There is no question about it—well-exercised people live longer, stay mentally alert for a longer time, have a better sex life into a far older age and have a generally much better appearance and a well-balanced personality. A study on persons older than 65 at Veterans Administration Hospital in Oregon has shown that patients without heart disease were physically very active throughout their lives (42).

What is good exercise routine? Run 5 miles a day? Swim a mile? Lift weights four times a week? NON-SENSE! Lots of people who want to stay in top shape do it without "killing" themselves; for the average person a much lighter program is sufficient. The important thing is to establish a *light* exercise program two or three times per week and to stick to it. Without exercise you will tire very easily, and there is a good chance that you will become quite unhappy with your sex life.

Hopefully you are convinced by now that you should do some exercise; now you should decide where, how, and when. Even the smallest towns have some kind of sports facilities, a swimming pool or a YMCA. If you live in or close to a bigger city, you can get a little fancier. Exercise, sports, and health clubs range in their fees from $100 per year up to $1000 or even more. The health club business is really booming; but before you sign up for a membership, check the following: Does the club have the facilities you want for your type of exercise, such as different exercise machines, swimming pool, whirl pool, sauna, steam room, sun and massage room? What type of membership do you want? Do you want to pay a higher initiation fee and a low yearly fee, or do you want a medium fee for every year? As a long term investment, the deal with the higher initiation fee is better because, etc. Find out if your club has facilities in other cities, or is associated with other clubs throughout the world. You might get transferred.

You don't want to join? Can't afford it? Well, don't give up, there are many kinds of exercise you can do indoors or outdoors. Indoors, first. Besides doing push-ups, hip-bends, sit-ups, knee-bends and running on the spot, you might get yourself an exercise manual such as *The Canadian Air Force Exercises*, or read the chapter on exercise in *The Sensuous Woman* or *The Sensuous Man*. Outdoors. try walking, bicycling, tennis, jogging, swimming, horseback riding or any sport or game that keep you somehow exercised.

The secret is to do all kinds of exercises. Exercise your whole body and not just your arms or your legs. Do your regular exercises at home or in your club; but whenever you feel like doing some others, do them. Different muscles are used for different movements or exercises; exercise all muscles from time to time. When should you exercise? Any time you have a chance. If you are at a beach, swim a while, don't just look at the water. If the weather is nice, go to work a few minutes earlier and walk an additional distance. If out with the kids, run a little. If your friends in the country have horses, don't just admire these beautiful animals, get on one—there should be one that fits your temperament. Go for a bicycle ride with your girlfriend or boyfriend; it's not only healthier, but cheaper than one-arm beer-lifting exercises.

Plan your exercises around your daily routine; do it at the right time and don't force it. For example: if you have plans for the evening and are already tired from work, don't try to sneak in an hour of exercise, just rest up a while. The next day you might not have any plans; visit your club and go through a good workout and get to bed early. Remember not to stuff yourself before exercising. Make sure that you get enough rest after you exercise. Give your body a chance to "do its thing." When you exercise, you burn up a lot of energy and your metabolism rate is increased tremendously. Oxidation products are accumulated in your cells, and you have to give your body a chance to get rid of them.

The metabolic products theory actually blames the

162

accumulation of oxidation products in our system for accelerating the aging process. There is definitely something to this theory, but I would rather classify it as a stress factor that contributes to aging. During sleep the metabolic rate is the slowest and that is the time when our system stabilizes itself by getting rid of all oxidation products and builds up energy reserves. If you overeat or sleep in a very hot room, your metabolic rate will be slightly higher and, as a result, all the biochemical reactions will continue at a higher rate, thus preventing the cleaning up process. The result is that you wake up tired. The important thing to remember is that it's your body; why hasten the aging process when the alternative is so easy?

A large research team, Per Björntop et al., compared the carbohydrate and lipid metabolism of middle-aged, physically well-trained men to the metabolism of randomly selected men of the same age group. A definite superiority of the well-trained men to the untrained men expressed itself in many biochemical reactions. Insulin was low, triglycerides were removed at a fast rate and fasting plasma lipids were low (139). Again you can see that physical exercise will improve your well-being. One day maybe you will be almost as fit as Mr. Lewis whom we all saw on television. Just in case you didn't: Mr. Lewis is 105 years old and runs six miles per day as exercise.

Running is an excellent exercise for keeping fit. For better results it should, however, be combined with some muscle-sport. A few years ago many people got on the jogging kick and many middle-aged and older men started dropping like flies. Naturally. They were untrained and tried to do much too much at one time.

HOW TO START RUNNING:
1) Find out the exact condition your body is in by having a physical.

2) For the first week do some extra walking at an accelerated pace; do slow jogging only sometimes, and only for 10 to 20 seconds at a time.

3) In the second week, besides the long distance walking, you can do some slow jogging. Only about twice, and for one minute each time.

4) After these first two weeks you can start jogging for about three or even five minutes and later you can increase the speed a little.

5) Never run right after a meal and never when you are already exhausted. Always rest up after exercise.

6) Combine your running with any other sport. You don't have to do one right after the other. I like to combine it with swimming, weight-lifting and other exercises that expand the chest and exercise arm muscles. Do only some light weight-lifting. Assuming you can lift a maximum of 150 pounds, you should exercise with a much lighter weight and do the exercise more often. Dr. Leaf, after visiting the areas where people were noted for long life spans, took up jogging himself.

Do you remember the Olympic Games? Wasn't it fascinating to watch what one can do with a human body? And it only takes a little effort to participate. We don't have to become Olympic competitors.

CHAPTER 18

Air Pollution—Do You Have A Chance?

"Most critical, of course, are the ill effects that air pollutants can have on people's health and well-being. Aside from the cost in physical misery, the monetary cost of respiratory illnesses that are exaggerated, if not actually caused by air pollution, may be well over $2 billion annually."

Dermot A. O'Sullivan
Bureau Head, San Francisco
Chemical and Engineering News
June 8, 1970.

Between 1969 and 1971, studies were carried out in Chicago, New York and other areas to determine the effect of pollution on our health. Dr. French, a government scientist, reported the results to an American Medical Association conference on air pollution in Chicago. The results showed clearly that there was a clear link between air pollution and respiratory diseases. People living in a highly polluted area showed a high risk of upper and lower respiratory disease. It was also found that children whose parents smoked were more strongly affected by pollution.

Living in Chicago I have recognized a clear improvement in the air quality in the last year. I am severely affected by pollution and I can literally predict the wind direction from the reactions of my nose and lungs. Whenever it's really bad, the wind comes from the south and covers Chicago with a layer of toxic fumes that can get me fuming too. I fail to see the reason that we should have to suffer because United States Steel or any one of the other polluters doesn't clean up the mess they are making or because the clean-up effort might affect their earnings. So next time you have the sniffles, check the wind direction and send a strong letter of protest in that direction and to your government agencies.

Air Pollution is defined as the addition of solid and gaseous materials to the atmosphere which can be injurious to our health. Air pollutants are solid particles such as smoke and dust, and gases such as carbon monoxide, sulfur dioxide, nitrogen oxides, hydrocarbons and several oxidation products of hydrocarbons. The balance between oxygen and carbon dioxide is normally kept constant by the following two processes: (a) In a process called photosynthesis plants use carbon dioxide and water, convert these with the help of chlorophyll and light energy from the sun into high energy carbohydrates, and give off oxygen. (b) Humans and other animals get energy by converting high energy carbohydrates into water and carbon dioxide.

Many other oxidation processes, such as the burning of gasoline, coal or any other fuel, form carbon dioxide. If the oxidation process is incomplete, then large quantities of carbon monoxide are formed. Carbon monoxide is an extremely poisonous gas, destroying cells when it reacts with our blood; we all know the dangers of carbon monoxide poisoning from automobile exhausts. The main sources of air pollution then are automobiles, industry, electricity suppliers, space heaters, and refuse burning. Since the subject of air pollution is deserving of a book itself, let's just concentrate here on how it affects our health and aging.

Air pollutants get into our system mainly through

the lungs. The substances of air pollution are as follows:

Solid Particles: Breathing in these particles is very much like smoking. Accumulation of solid particles in the lungs will decrease the oxygen/carbon dioxide exchange. Chemically these particles are often carcinogenic, causing the formation of lung cancer.

Sulfur dioxide: It reacts with the moisture of the lungs to form sulfurous acid and can destroy proteins. Even if an acid is neutralized, it is still in our system and puts extra stress on cells. We learned in an earlier chapter that any unusual stress increases the aging rate.

Professor L. Schneider of the University of Arizona has presented evidence that white blood cells are damaged by sulfur dioxide. He bubbled air containing very little sulfur dioxide (as low as 5.7 parts per million) through blood cell cultures and found that fewer cells synthesized DNA and that these cells were also smaller than cells in cultures through which pure air was bubbled. Besides this, about 20% of the cells showed chromosome damage (72).

Nitrogen oxides: Nitrogen oxides can also react with moisture to form acids; therefore, we have basically the same effect here as with sulfur dioxide. The major danger of nitrogen oxides is the formation of radicals. The damaging effect of these reactive particles to our cells was discussed in Chapter 5 and in more detail in Chapter 20. The formation of nitrogen oxides occurs in the hot automobile engines, while gasoline is oxidized with air in the engine.

Hydrocarbons: Hydrocarbons in the air come from unburned or only partially burned automobile fuels. A number of complicated reactions take place among the hydrocarbons, nitrogen oxides, oxygen and sunlight. These reactions form *ozone* and oxidation products of hydrocarbons. A dramatic increase in the

167

number of radicals resulting from exposure to large quantities of ozone is a well-established fact.

B. Goldstein and H. Demopolous have demonstrated that radicals are formed by the interaction of linoleic acid (a fatty acid in our bodies and ozone (73). For example, the ozone level in Los Angeles is approximately 0.2 ppm (parts per million) and has reached levels up to 0.6. About 10 ppm can kill small animals (19). Vitamin E, a radical interceptor, can protect small animals from such high ozone levels. All this fits very nicely into the new radical theory about aging.

If you know a little chemistry you might want to read W. Pryor's article on "Radical Pathology" in *Chemical and Engineering News,* June 7, 1971. Professor E. Stephens of the University of California has shown that not only animals, but also plants, are affected by the oxidation products of air pollution in concentrations down to the parts-per-hundred million levels.

An increased death rate from coronary heart disease due to air pollution factors was also observed by W. Winkelstein of the University of California (74).

Since it will probably be quite a while before the air is pure again, you have to face the facts of today and decide what you can do to protect yourself from the effects of air pollution. You could move to an area of low air pollution, but this solution doesn't seem to be a very reasonable alternative for many of us. A less expensive step would be to equip your home with an air purifier and have it running whenever the pollution level is high. But make sure that the purifier is a good instrument that doesn't generate ozone (this sometimes happens with less expensive electronic air purifiers).

There are still other indications that better living through chemistry could come from the antioxidant group of Dr. Passwater's research with test animals. He has subjected test animals to high concentrations of air pollution and measured the death rate of the animals. When they were fed some of the drugs that are presently being tested as youth drugs (see Chapter 14), it was found that these animals survived even extremely high air pollution levels (71).

Pollution in general should be of major concern to all of us. Even though large companies constantly let us know in television commercials how concerned they are about the environment, what they are really doing about cleaning up this earth is merely a fraction of what they could do. We have the most beautiful country and look how we mess it up. If any public relations man from a large company tells you that it is impossible to clean up the mess they make, this is a lot of nonsense. We have the know-how and several companies already specialize in pollution-controlling devices. All it takes is a little money. One lousy cent of every share of stock in every company in addition to the efforts being made right now could solve the entire pollution problem. Large numbers of animals are still being affected by pollution right in front of our eyes and we don't seem to get this message. Thank god, the cancer risk of high-flying SST airplanes was recognized early enough. The biggest air polluters are automobiles. A simple legislative step, namely to assure that every automobile owner has the ignition system and the pollution devices checked at least once a year would solve part of the problem. We could build smaller automobiles with smaller engines. It is almost a joke to build cars with 400-horsepower engines if the maximum speed limit is 65 mph. And where do you ever use the so-often advertised tremendous acceleration of your car? The energy crisis might lead us in the right direction. Gasoline price increases, I believe, have merely started. We will therefore have to think about buying smaller cars which give us better mileage and which also burn less fuel and therefore decrease the pollution level. Catalytic converters can also be installed easily in any automobile and reduce pollution levels. Maybe we should even give some credit to people that install these devices voluntarily. But this is just a transition state to the real thing, the electrical automobile which is already waiting to go into mass production. These cars, as of 4 years ago, were already able to go at speeds of up to 120 mph and had a radius of 80 miles. Recent improvements in electrical energy storage cells should improve the above data by at least 25 per cent. Imagine, all you have to do in the evening is plug your auto into some electricity outlet or when you park your car somewhere you add another dime to the parking meter to get a quick re-charge. In some countries where it gets extremely cold in the winter, parking meters have electrical outlets so that you can plug in a heater to keep the engine warm. Our nuclear reactors can supply us with more electricity than we need. These new reactors are of the breeder-type. That means that they actually produce nuclear fuel. We can also already recognize the effects of ocean pollution on animals. Our oceans are immense food reservoirs and look how we are destroying them.

Help Preserve our environment! Write to your Government representatives.

PART V

Conclusions

Estimates by several researchers in the aging field predict that it will soon be possible to increase our efficiency tremendously and lengthen our average life span by 40 to 50 healthy years.

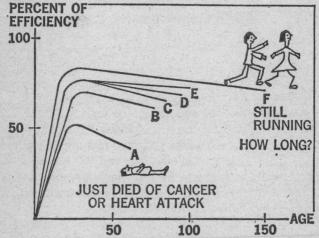

Figure B

You determine which performance curve you would like to have. You might reach 100% if you were perfect in every area. But who wants to be perfect?

In Chapter 2 we defined aging as a constant loss of cells—a fact well agreed on by the experts. The importance of keeping each single cell functioning as long as possible is necessary for two reasons: (1) Old cells show a decrease in efficiency and (2) normal efficient cells have only a limited number of cell divisions. It is therefore important to eliminate as many factors as possible that make cells age.

There are several major causes for aging; it is an extremely complex process. Some of the changes in our system that represent aging are accumulation of oxidation products, damage to the DNA, the decrease of RNA in older age, damage to the cell walls and all the other materials in our cells and the formation of large cross-linked molecules in the entire system.

Two major theories that deal with the causes of aging are the "cross-link theory" and the "free radical theory." One can almost say that these two theories are one because Bjorksten proposed that free radicals were one cause of cross-linking. It just appears that free radicals cause a larger percentage of the cell damage than was believed previously.

What is most convincing about the free radicals is that a follow-up already led to a 166% prolongation of the average life span of test animals (71). A strong decrease in the incidence of cancer was also observed in these test animals. Chapter 19 contains the views of Dr. Passwater in his own words; he also discusses some of his test results with antioxidants. Science has established the fact that it is possible to extend the human life span, regardless of whether the free radical theory is correct or not. Since the metabolism of these test animals in respect to aging and metabolism is similar to ours, it is unnecessary to speculate a lot and we come up with a possible human life which is more than 120 to 130 years. Some of these experiments actually indicate that it will be possible to go past the maximum possible life span of a species. But this is still speculative and we'll just have to wait and see. More important, all these experiments show that it is possible to stay physically fit and mentally alert for a longer time period of our total life.

Now we know that it is possible to extend our average life expectancy and stay physically fit and mentally alert into a much older age. But how about our youthful appearance? Well, if we slow down the aging process that just means that we stay younger longer. We have also seen that some therapies like the nucleic acid therapy make a person look younger. If this is not yet enough, you can get an even more youthful look through youth surgery. A painless 30-minute procedure which decreases the size of your aging nose a little bit can already make you look 15 years younger. So you can see that it will be easy for a 60-year-old to look like 35 or for a 75-year-old to look like a 45-year-old.

Personally, I will not worry too much about looking a few years younger as long as I have a well-functioning body and brain.

Let's examine a few efficiency curves again. Curve A in Figure 11 shows the efficiency curve for an average person who does not know the "ABC's" of good nutrition, does not have a well-planned exercise program, smokes more than 20 cigarettes per day, lives in an area of high pollution, does not get enough rest and does not take any drug compounds to slow down the aging process.

Let's take a look at Mr. A. in Figure B. A person who "breaks all the rules" will probably have an average life expectancy of 60 years with a maximum performance when he (or she) is 25 years old. According to our theory a good exercise program will raise his efficiency and prolong his life span so that we get to curve B. Good nutrition in respect to our biochemical processes was discussed in Chapter 4. Curve C will be the result of this improvement. If we want to reach the end of our curve, we have to make sure that we don't die from the effects of cigarette smoking before we get there; an average life span increase will lead us to curve D. Eliminating the stress and aging effects of air pollution brings us up to curve E. "Youth Drugs" or their basic chemicals taken separately will extend life expectancy to 120 or more years. Finally, we have arrived at our ideal curve F which stands for your FUTURE.

It should be emphasized again that it is not necessary to become a health nut; "doing almost everything right" in these different areas is relatively easy and was discussed in the preceding chapters. Aging is an accumulation of many different factors. That is the reason why improvement in one area might help a little but will not have a dramatic effect.

It is difficult to rate these different areas and to assign a priority to each one of them. The life style, physical activity, surroundings, eating habits and stress factors will change from person to person so that it is impossible to work out an order of priorities for "the average person." A business man who sits all day in his chair, meets his clients over a martini at lunch and constantly worries about fulfilling his commitments will have a completely different set of priorities than a sculptor who works hard with his hands and who is quite content with his life.

By reading the chapters on the various topics you will have to decide yourself where you have to change a lot or a little.

However, from my surveys of many students it seems that more than 80% needed some real changes in the areas of smoking, exercise and nutrition. Are you different?

And another topic, stress, needs some special attention. As Dr. Hans Selye, the No. 1 authority on stress factors, has shown, stress is a major factor in aging. At the University of Montreal Dr. Selye has discovered that our body has several defense mechanisms against stress which are controlled by the adrenal hormones. Psychological stress is often more difficult than physical stress or stress put on our system by toxic materials. Stress decreases your body's defenses, it can make you sick, give you ulcers and heart attacks.

Why is this so? Mainly because we don't know how to cope with stress or because we put more stress on our system than we can handle. Since stress affects each one of us differently we have to determine our own limits for stress and act accordingly. When counteracting the effects of stress you will sometimes have to make serious decisions. Just don't underestimate the effects of stress.

If your boss gives you ulcers and you can't cope with this situation then quit and find yourself another job.

Does your wife (or husband, or girlfriend, or boyfriend) constantly make life hell for you? Well then, tell them where to get off, or bid them goodbye.

Let me give you an example of how I solved a friend's stress situation very successfully:

Mr. F. had heard that I was working in the health

field and asked me for urgently needed advice. He explained his situation. He lived in the big city and had a very high paying job about 40 minutes from where he lived. He therefore had to get up as early as 6 AM to fight the highway traffic in his new expensive car. He returned between 6 and 7 in the evening, often bringing work home. He knew a little about nutrition and ate a good meal every evening about 7:30. His girl friend was quite patient with him, but wasn't very happy because he was always tired and run down so that he wasn't really good for anything. When I asked him if he had an exercise program or belonged to a health club he just shook his head and said that he used to be quite active but now just didn't have the time for it. At his job he was quite capable but he had the kind of boss who would push his employes to the limit in order to get his money's worth. He didn't refer to his boss by name, but as "the bastard." A company in the city had offered him a job which he liked but he just couldn't decide to take a $350 per month salary cut (and I agreed that was a large cut). After evaluating his situation and the results of a physical by his doctor it was quite clear to me what his problems were: too little time to recover from his job, lack of sleep, nervousness and a generally unhealthy life style. Since he was really sick of this life he made some drastic changes: He quit his job and took the job in the city. Since he only needed a car to go to work, he sold his and started taking the subway to work. On weekends he rented cars. Since his car cost him approximately $320 per month (everything included), this was equal to approximately $550 taxable salary in his tax bracket. He could spend $150 on public transportation, car rentals and taxis, and still come out ahead. He was now able to sleep 1½ hours longer in the morning, go for a nice breakfast at a nearby diner and still get to work on time. He now had his big meal in the middle of the day in the company of friends who worked in the same area and arrived home about one hour earlier. He still didn't like his new boss but he was able to communicate with him and that relaxed him quite a bit. He also joined a health club which was about half way between his home and work and could be reached by a 15 minute walk from either location. After 4 weeks he was a changed man. Certainly dozens of small factors had contributed to a highly stressed situation. Knowing about the facts of stress helped change this man's life.

And again: don't underestimate the effects of stress.

If it comes to taking large doses of vitamins such as C, E, A and the B-complex, advice is still difficult to give. Even though I take them and don't know of any research results that suggest that you shouldn't, I still feel that more research results are needed. Careful with vitamin A; it's good but too much can actually lead to vitamin A poisoning.

If you take nucleic acids you have to drink a lot of liquids because the metabolites are acidic compounds which have to be neutralized and washed out of your system. You should not do this too often because too much liquids will offset the salt balance and buffer systems in your body.

And the future is for us—the people that live now. Within one or two years science will know much more about the factors that accelerate the aging process. Tables of compounds listing wrong nutrients, drugs, preservatives, household chemicals and pollutants will be publicly available to warn us of their potential danger. A national institute of aging is already in the first stages. Money from the government will help to accelerate research on human aging. There are also many medical journals that specialize in reporting results in this field and which you might consult.

There is no doubt that we will find drugs that will do a better job than the antioxidants now in use. This has happened before. Natural products isolated from plants or other living matter were impoved by chemists by changing the structure just a little bit. It is a simple task for a chemist to take an active compound and literally make hundreds of derivatives. And tests are already being developed that will test the effectiveness of these youth drugs in a short time. When the synthetic chemist goes to work, he will find less expensive processes for making these drugs.

Thousands of volunteers will be needed to test these new drugs. Maybe you want to participate? You can bet that I will. In the meantime a lot can be done. At first we can improve our physical fitness and mental alertness and raise our efficiency curves close to the maximum. By acting reasonably in accordance with the material discussed in Chapters 4, 8, 14, 15 and 16, you can lengthen your average life span up to 36 years.

We have seen in the previous chapters that there are many ways to extend the average life expectancy of test animals. All of the following have shown in separate tests that it was possible to extend the average life expectancy of test animals: excellent nutrition, antioxidant therapy, nucleic acid therapy, pantothenic acid, immunosuppressive compounds, cell shots and exercise. How long would it be possible to extend the average life expectancy if one would treat some animals with all these compounds? I hope that some of my own experiments will show that. We are trying to get as close to natural conditions as possible where the results on test animals could lead our way. We are also not using any compounds that could be harmful to our system. In one experiment we use four sets of mice:

Group 1) Standard environment and foods.
Group 2) Improved environment; exercise wheels, nucleic acid shots to revitalize the major organs.
Group 3) Improved environment; exercise wheels, nucleic acid shots to revitalize the endocrine system.
Group 4) Improved invironment; exercise wheels, nucleic acid shots, vitamin C, pantothenic acid, niacin amide, procaine hydrochloride, brewers yeast, wheat germ.

In this experiment we are working with retired breeders (white mice). This experiment simulates real life and we are trying to find out to what degree life extensions are possible on a middle aged being.

The experiment is still in progress. As of this date about 50% of the control animals have died. All the treated animals are still alive and look good. This already represents quite an extension of the average life span above normal.

In another experiment we used retired breeders (rats). When you work with rats you have problems doing longevity studies because these animals grow sometimes immense tumors. Eight rats received standard foods and eight rats received everything the fourth group of mice (see above) received. Seven of the control animals have already grown tumors. No tumors were found in the treated group.

I have about 30 different experiments running at the same time where we try to pinpoint possible rejuvenations a little more precisely. In some experiments I am working with methods that are really far out, but I believe that it is a little too early to talk about these experiments.

For older people and people who want to reverse

the aging process our hopes are with researchers like Dr. Bjorksten. His research objective, the removal of aging damage, was considered impossible a few years ago, but Dr. Bjorksten has shown that he is on the right track.

Middle-aged and older people often believe that it is too late to start a new, healthy life. Heavy smokers believe that it isn't worth it to quit smoking; they believe that the damage is already done—so why quit? WRONG. In a recent study three large groups of people were compared. Non-smokers, heavy smokers and heavy smokers that had quit cigarette smoking at least six months ago. There was literally no difference between non-smokers and heavy smokers that had quit smoking. Only the people that kept puffing showed all the ill effects of cigarette smokers. So it *is* worth it to quit or at least to cut down before it really is too late.

Money is a big problem and research could be accelerated immensely if it were not for a lack of financial support. There are hundreds of excellent researchers without a good job. We have the manpower, the know-how and the instrumentation necessary but we don't put all this to use because there is so little money available. Do you know what a donation of $1 per person in this country could do? We could establish research centers on aging. Each center could have $3 million for buildings and equipment. Twenty professional and 40 technical people in each center could be financed with this money for five years. Human aging research could be accelerated tremendously. It is all in your hands—money and the power to tell your government representatives that you want more research done in this area.

In the meantime I will be in contact with the researchers in every country who work in human aging research and each year I will revise my book to bring

181

you up to-date with the latest research results and facts on how the aging process can be slowed down. I would also appreciate any comments on what you would like to know in greater detail.

But there are several other areas where we have to change our attitude completely. Nowadays many people feel that when retirement age comes around, they are too old for anything but sitting around and waiting for the end. The way it should actually be, is to have some kind of transition from work to retirement. A large number of people just can't handle that sudden change from work to no work and lots of time. I know it sounds ridiculous, but that's the way it is. One way to solve this problem would be to give people more and more free time as they near retirement age. At that time they might work only half-time or maybe only three weeks per month. Retirement, or better the end of the work period of your life should be something to look forward to—a reward for the slave labor during the past years. Now you have time to do things you always wanted to do and since you kept yourself physically fit and mentally alert, you also have the capacity to do so. Sleep long in the morning until you are well rested, meet a friend for breakfast at a nice place, go for a long walk at the lake or in the park. You might go for a swim at your club, exercise a little, get a massage, see a new Renoir exhibition that just opened at the art museum and many universities teach very interesting subjects that are not for young students only. Why not remodel your apartment or house? Or you can finally get around to building your own weekend A-frame in the country. Travel around and see what a beautiful world we live in. You don't think so? Well, then help to improve it, just don't sit around doing nothing. Have you ever visited London, Berlin, Munich, Cairo, Delhi or Tokyo?

When I did some sky diving, I met a man who had

just retired and was now taking sky diver lessons. He told me that he always wanted to try it but never had the time. When my interest in this new hobby wanes, he told me, I will go to the Grand Cayman Islands and learn how to scuba dive.

Naturally all this costs money and we should plan and save some so that we are not stuck with all the free time and no resources to do something with it. Whenever we work, a certain amount of money should be taken out automatically so that sufficient money is available in old age to pay for the minimum requirements. Besides this, each one of us should plan and save so that sufficient funds are available in later years. Wouldn't it be nice to have, let's say, an extra 50 thousand dollars when you retire? But where shall we get it from? Relatively easy. Let's assume you are 30 years old and buy two packs of cigarettes per day. At first you improve your health, decrease your chance of dying from cancer, heart attack or emphysema by giving up smoking and then invest the money you save every year in a special retirement fund. Know how much money you will have at age 60? Approximately 50 to 60 thousand dollars if you get approximately 8% on your money; and every financial advisor will tell you that that is not too difficult.

And relax, take it easy and love your neighbor. With a little patience and determination we can even change the attitude of this country where even a gasoline and a cough drop can hate.

We live in the richest and most resourceful country on this earth and we can afford to honor and value the old people who have made this country great. Treat and respect the old as you will want to be treated when you are old.

CHAPTER 19

The Views of Six Experts on Health and Aging

Dr. R. Passwater's statement on health and aging:

At this time, antioxidant therapy is just beginning to reveal its potential to better human life. While attention has been focused on increasing human life span, antioxidant therapy has been proving effective in preventing diseases such as cancer and atherosclerosis. Our research has significantly extended the life spans of our laboratory animals, but more importantly we have observed true evidence of slowing the aging process, such as activity, ability to fight viral infections and absence of physical aging signs. The absence of cancers and low incidence of tumors in general was at first a pleasant surprise. Later, evidence emerged that free radicals were involved in the initiation of cancers by carcinogens, and we pursued this link with excellent results. As an example antioxidant therapy reduces the incidence of cancer in laboratory animals caused by certain carcinogens from 80 to 100% to 0 to 20%.

As you can see, our research has not been confined to adding years of life, but adding life to years as well. We are attacking three main areas; and we place emphasis in the following order. First, preventing debilitation from chronic diseases; second, allowing nearly everyone to reach the present maximum life span and third, to actually extend human life span. Eventually a fourth goal, rejuvenation, will be added to our goals. This goal is no longer a wild dream. Already researchers such as Bjorksten are pioneering this area.

There are steps everyone can take today to live better longer. Don't smoke, be happy, eat a diversified diet and keep active. Antioxidant therapy, when available, will help in each case. The evils of smoking are well known, but the relationship of personality, life style and nutrition to life span are not understood by the average person. Even when understood, the average person tends to ignore them; then when it is too late to pay attention, they are sorry.

Personality is important, because those people who have reached very old age and who have been studied intensely, showed only one major trait in common. They enjoyed life. Their minds were on today, not yesterday. They had an optimistic outlook and a wonderful sense of humor.

Life style is second in importance. You have to be active, physically and mentally. Physical activity (as opposed to regimented exercise) is a must. Walk instead of riding, run instead of walking and never use an elevator. Playing ping-pong while watching TV. Never just lie around.

Nutrition is ranked third here but it really is a part of personality and life style. Active people who enjoy life always see that they eat for health. Proper nutrition prevents the wasting and crippling diseases of old age. The only way to ensure good nutrition is to eat a balanced and diversified diet, with caloric intake equal to expended calories. New vitamins are still being discovered, so we don't know everything about food or requirements. Eat non-processed foods whenever possible. Add more natural bulk to your diet. Take vitamin supplements (especially E, C and B complex). You can ignore the pollution in food if your diet is diversified enough not to eat too much of one food.

Soon antioxidant therapy will be proven, and its benefits available to everyone. Meanwhile protect yourself with good nutrition and natural antioxidants.

Dr. Hermann Hoepke, Professor of Medicine in Heidelberg, author of many research papers in the field of radiation therapy, cancer research and cell therapy talks about fresh cell therapy and aging:

All living beings constantly create for themselves appropriate internal and external living conditions. Nevertheless, they age and must die. However, death is not caused because the ability to create appropriate living conditions diminishes and ultimately ceases. Likewise, neither the wear and tear of single parts of the body and its organs, nor the accumulation of harmful compounds are the cause of aging and death. Rather, it is caused by the fact that damaged, worn and aged parts are not repaired and replaced and harmful components are not removed.

Recent research is making it increasingly clear that the cause of aging must lie in the structure of the nuclei. By the process of aging we mean the characteristics, i.e. the symptoms of aging and the changes which can be found in all cells and tissues. For example, the skin changes its color, turgor and elasticity. The speed of nerve pulse transmissions decreases, the amount of air inhaled and exhaled diminishes, while the flow of blood through the kidneys as well as its flow of plasma, decrease and the filtration rate declines. The decline in performance of all organs is approximately 0.5 to 1.3% per year (Strehler, 1968).

We also know that changes due to aging do not occur uniformly and simultaneously in all organs. In weighing human organs, the following observations can be made: The brain attains its maximum weight during the second decade of life; the spleen during the third and the bone structure during the fourth.

Muscles and liver are heaviest during the fifth and heart and lungs during the eighth decade of life. Comparing the weight of these organs with the body weight, we find that the weight of the brain has already reached its peak during the first decade as has that of the liver and kidneys. Thus, heart, arteries and lungs exhibit the longest period of growth, that of intestines being somewhat shorter; muscles, liver, bones and kidney cease growth early; brain and eyes are the first to terminate growth (Mühlmann, 1925). Thus, the process of aging begins quite early, in fact, one might say with the first cell division.

Life and death belong together and the beginning of life is the beginning of the aging process. Aging is a "biomorphosis," a change continuing throughout life, and irreversible alteration of living substances as a function of time (Bürger, 1958). In the microscopic realm we are familiar with physical-chemical changes of colloids within the cells and the intercellular substances as well as a diminution of its water retention ability.

However, these are merely the characteristics of the aging process—what causes it?

All research points towards a morphological or chemical explanation which must lie in the structure of the nuclei.

As early as 1921 Doms pointed out that every cell basically carries all the characteristics of its species. But not every cell can, during its life span, develop its entire potential. Only the sperm cells are capable of doing that. In all other cells, as for example in the gland or nerve cells, a large percentage of their actual potential remains inactive. The aging process of cells lies in the contrast between activated potential and potential that remains inactive.

This concept of cell potential while not scientifically comprehensible, has attained visible form through new research. Curtis, like Doms, has recognized that always only a fraction of available genetic information is utilized. On the morphological level the following can be observed with increasing age: abnormal chromosomes on many cells, pieces broken off, deformations and deviations from the gene-chain. These abnormal chromosomes could cause the formation of substances that interfere with the normal processes and therefore accelerate aging. Hahn, another scientist, also believes that such substances could accumulate during the course of life and can cause aging and senility (Strehler, 1968).

An effective therapy of aging must try to prevent these changes of the nuclei. In 1936 P. Niehans discovered that cell therapy is capable of doing just that. In 1909 the American scientist A. Carell showed that aging tissue cultures could be revitalized by adding the substances of young cells. And that's how cell therapy works. It wants to add vitality to weakened, damaged or older organisms by adding the substances of embryonic cells. Halstedt, another American scientist, recognized that an organism tolerates transplanted cells and its immunologic defenses remain silent if its organs need these transplants in order to regenerate a disturbed system. Aging cells need the full potential of embryonic cells and this way they can get it. We know that the young implanted cells are quickly broken into their components. These are picked up by the cells that need them—in this case by the aging cells.

Cell therapy is therefore a biological therapy.

Murphi and Danchakoff and especially Paul Weiss and his students deserve credit for their important work in this field. Their work has proven that implantations of embryonic cells cause specific growth reactions in the corresponding organs of the recipient of these cells.

The most extensive scientific work in cell therapy was performed by Kment in 1963. He has proven the effects of embryonic cells on aging tissue by exact measurements. At first he measured the exact effect of aging on the tissue, organs and organ functions of rats. Then he was able to measure exactly the extent of the revitalization process. In all experiments a definite increase of the vitality was observed after the injection of cells from testes or placenta. The overall condition of the animals was improved clearly by an improvement of elementary functions so that it was also possible to withstand damaging effects more easily. The decrease of the vitality due to aging was clearly slowed down.

Since it is not possible to describe all of Kment's experiments in detail only the most important results will be discussed:

After implantation of testes or placenta cells the respiration of heart, liver and kidney was increased so that it corresponded much more to the respiration of younger animals (for embryonic connective tissue cells the results were the same). All these measurements were done with homogenates of these cells in the Warburg-apparatus. When the locomotive activity of senile rats was measured using exercise drums, the treated animals showed a definite improvement which lasted ten days.

The memory of rats that had to find their food in a complicated labyrinth was also clearly improved. When the animals were tested after two 12-day pauses, the treated animals were definitely faster and made fewer mistakes. The collagen fibers of the connective tissue, which we find in all organs, normally get more rigid and shorter in the aging process; it can lead to serious illnesses like arthritis, rheumatism and scleroses. After treatment with cells the fibers showed the characteristics of younger animals. The shortening took place later.

The resistance of the skin to laceration which normally decreases with age, was increased by cell therapy. The skin remained stronger. Characteristics of aging in the aorta appeared later. Summarizing: Whatever the tissue and organs examined, the results were always the same. After treatment with testes or placenta cells the signs of aging appeared later. The aging process was slowed down.

Implanted embryonic connective tissue cells from the navel string and hypodermis connective tissue are of special importance since they revitalize and activate the immunological and defense system (the reticulo-endothelial system) of our body which was demonstrated in my own experiments. Lymphocytes, plasma cells, fat cells and also mast cells are formed at an increased rate. And those are the cells that destroy cancer (Kidd and Toolan, 1950, Hoepk 1954, Landsberger 1959-69). Through revitalization and strengthening of the defensive tissue, cell therapy becomes cancer therapy. While the chemical therapy wants to destroy cancer cells selectively, which has not yet been possible to achieve, the cell therapy strengthens the body characteristic defenses via the connective tissue. With a combination of embryonic connective tissue cells and Heparinoid—which is contained in fat cells and destroys cancer cells selectively (Landsberger)—the growth of different types of tumors slowed down or completely stopped. Blumberg has also treated patients with serious carcinoms which were treated without success with other methods, and removed metastases and achieved long lasting results.

The resistance of the aging organism can be strengthened by vitamins, exercise and no smoking.

All these steps are important but only treat the symptoms of aging.

One can fight infectious diseases with drugs, vitamin C, cataplasm and baths. But the most effective method is to fight the cause, the bacteria with antibiotics like sulfonamids and penicillin.

To fight cancer with chemical means alone has not yet been successful. The cell therapy fights the cause of aging. It can be combined with other chemical and physical methods.

As yet, no therapy can free us from aging and death but we can decrease the effects of aging. Cell therapy gives old cells new vitality and works the best in a body that is strengthened by a healthy life style.

Dr. Orzechowski is Professor of Medicine in Cologne, Germany, specializing in nucleic acid research; Dr. Orzechowski's views on how to deal with the aging problem:

Many theories on aging have appeared but most of them are already out-dated and useless. They just don't fit in with our modern ways of thinking which are based on the facts of the natural sciences. Today we are more concerned with DNA and RNA. We also know more about the metabolic processes, the lysomes and the accumulation of metabolic products in the cells. The belief that aging is a loss of information on a molecular basis fits better into our new ways of thinking. One theory on aging where aging is a programmed process, deals with the planned turning on and off of certain regulatory genes, determining the course of life for some species.

And with this we touch on certain properties of the DNA. The DNA is one of the largest bio-molecules we know; the molecular weight is estimated to be more than 10^8 (which is 100,000,000). Such gigantic molecules will not be able to pass through the pores of the membranes of the cell nucleus. The entire mass which carries the hereditary factors remain locked in the nucleus. Therefore it is also difficult to imagine a replacement of damaged DNA; it belongs with the futuristic dreams of a genetical engineer. The findings that DNA of aging animals is hardly changed also fits nicely into this picture.

However, it is different with the RNA. We remember the reports that the RNA content of human cells increases up to the age of 40 and then continuously decreases. Speaker, who treated older people regularly with yeast RNA, found that their appetites increased, they slept better and their general well-being increased.

We can be certain that the intensity of the protein synthesis depends on the age of a person. Here, for biochemical reasons, we also have to expect the largest wear and tear: The protein synthesis is the most important performance of the cell; it uses almost 90% of all the cell's available energy. For synthesis we expand only 2.5% for the DNA, 3.1% for the RNA, 3.7% for the lipids and 2.7% for the polysaccharides, which represents only a small percentage of the entire expanded energy. One has also found that the protein synthesis in three-day-old rats is five times as high as in fully grown animals. Robertson, Gardner and others were able to extend the life span of rats seven to 17% with yeast RNA. According to Satake, an increase in the vitality runs parallel to the increase in the RNA metabolism. Jarlstedt and Steward found that the RNA in interstitial rat cells was increased whenever signs of a special biological activity were recognized; the RNA content decreased whenever the activity ceased. According to Solyom, the RNA does not possess any special, pharmacologically stimulating action, which we wouldn't really expect anyway. That we are dealing here with processes of general biological importance we can also see by comparative studies with plants. When working with seedlings of plants (lens culinaris), Pilet recognized that the RNA content in old cells was only about half as much as in young cells. Here we also recognize another biochemical fact: the activity of RN-ase was significantly higher in old cells than in young cells.

Dyckerhoff introduced the RNA as Regeneresen[R] into the therapy. For geriatric needs Dyckerhoff prepared a mixture of RNA from placenta, testes, ovaries, hypothalamus, adrenal cortex, pituitary gland, thalamus, spleen, vascular wall, cerebral cortex, liver, kidney and yeast; this is the special preparation RN-13. This preparation has been tested in Paris by Dr. Wentz in a double blind study. Besides the improvements that were already noted by Cameron and others for the RNA, the Parisian doctor found an increase in the plasma proteins as a measure of the stimulation of the protein synthesis.

Benjamin S. Frank, M.D., the originator of the nucleic acid therapy, was in Portugal at the time but has responded to my request for his views of aging in a letter which reads as follows:

I have been experimenting with nucleic acids since 1961 systematically and did other work of a similar kind even before this. I believe that I am the originator of the use of nucleic acids in the therapy of aging and many degenerative diseases. My early work also carried me into a study of the various physiologic effects of RNA and RNA+DNA in living mammals and man, including the discovery of their 1) antianoxia effect, 2) anti low temperature and freezing effects—survival in a wider range of low (and high) temperatures, 3) antigrowth or growth-inhibiting effects, 4) antiaging effect, 5) antivival effect, 6) energizing effects, etc. These effects were seen during or prior to 1961 by me, described in a then dated patent application; many papers and in book form in 1964 in *A New Approach to Degenerative Disease and Aging,* subtitled "Effects of RNA, DNA with other metabolites." This was the first book published on the subject. The articles, books, etc. from the beginning delineated clearly a theory, not just a compilation of observations: namely, that nucleic acids, nucleosides, etc., when absorbed, injected, or taken orally by an animal (or human) have as the main result of their cellular activity the marked increase of homeostatically appropriate enzyme synthesis and/or activation of a wide range. The exact direction and degree of this synthesis and activation are governed to a great degree not only by the preceding state of the cell, but also by the associated coenzymes (vitamins) and cofactors (minerals) and substrates present or administered concurrently with the nucleic acids or derivatives. It is precisely this latter point that should show us the way to direct (i.e. significantly control) the direction and result of metabolism in desired or needed ways. This is my most basic tenet, and in more modern terms, it has later been partially subsumed under the heading of "orthomolecular medicine," which of course refers to vitamins primarily. In my earlier and still extant view it is not any one or few things, but a whole system of metabolites which is active here in "RNA therapy," which is an unfortunate term, for it does not evoke an image of this system of metabolites which is active. Of course the nucleic acids are the most critical cornerstone of this "system," or should I rather say "directed metabolic system, containing nucleic acids."

Thus with this approach, it should be possible, by activation and synthesis of proper enzymes to repair various kinds of cellular and sub-cellular damage with some degree of precision, too. This is a point which no one working with nucleosides, nucleic acids etc. has properly developed. It also greatly helps explain why DNA, damaged in degenerative diseases and aging is repaired by the type of nucleic acid therapy I espouse. Indeed, not only are the nucleic acid of DNA repair enzymes synthesized and activated, but this will be even better accomplished when more is known of the loci of damage in DNA and its associated chemicals, for we can then give substrates involved in these damaged loci, and of course any coenzymes or cofactors known to be involved in reactions occuring normally there with these substrates.

I believe one clinical case, typical of many others, can be mentioned to illustrate this point of a "directed metabolic system" in a rather gross clinical sense.

A woman of middle age, mid-sixties, came to me with a foot drop of many months duration. She had been given B_{12} and B_1 and B complex injections to no avail, by other physicians. On examination she was found to have spinal compass and arthritis in the lower spine (I am writing of it) without notes or case history etc., only otherwise in fairly good health, be the cause. DNA in moderately high doses, multi- and was one, inositol, and a higher than average vita diet, for one month. This gave no help. was given lactose (i.e. galactose) 1½ tea- 3 times daily and within 2-3 days the foot drop had gone nearly completely. It is my opinion (and this was the rationale for use of lactose) that the galactose would be used to build up cerebrosides— build up myelin. This appeared to be very likely. The rapid improvement, also seen in other neurologic cases, tends to show that this approach did work, and that by

195

use of a proper substrate along with the nucleic acids etc., a chemical damage was repaired.

Of course, I then proceeded to treat her spine problem which was the original cause, but the above is what I mean by a "directed metabolic system".

One experiment I have not yet included in my book involves 10 albino mice, 22 months old, given injections (subcutaneous) every other day for 6 days of a formula containing the following:

nucleocides:
ATP 0.2 mg
GTP 0.2 mg
UTP 0.2 mg
CTP 0.2 mg
TMP 0.3 mg

vitamins, coenzymes:
¼ amounts listed in book
Nucleic Acid Therapy of Aging and Degenerative Disease on page 105

minerals:
KCL 0.2 mg
NaCl 0.4 mg
KL 0.02 mcg
Mn Citrate 0.12 mg
Ca gluconate 1 mg
Mg gluconate 0.2 mg
Zn lactate 0.2 mg

amino acids:
½ amounts listed on
page 105 of same book

sugars:
glucose 25 mg
ribose 5 mg

Also given were: organ specific RNA's from liver extraction: liver, spleen, kidneys, brain, heart, 0.3 mg each, and DNA from rat liver 0.5 mg.

The effects of this (metabolic) system on aged mice was more dramatic than anything observed in prior experiments, done without organ specific RNA and DNA. The activity of these old mice increased markedly and the hair became soft, clean, fine in first week following injections. Ten control mice of same age, physical condition, died within 2–5 weeks of beginning of experiment. These mice lived 6–8 months (mean 7.2 month) on same diet as controls, which was a good standard diet for mice.

This work shows the importance of a "directed metabolic system with nucleic acids" in the attack on aging. It is precisely this sort of thing that I am planning to elaborate on in my next work, and to develop as soon as possible into an injectable for humans. The word directed is not fully appropriate here, for I have not specifically included those exact substrates singularly involved (except for the nucleosides) in the defects of the cell due to aging, but have rather attacked these defects generally. Were a specific lipid or sugar involved, I would have used these or their precursors, in addition to the rest of the formula. precursors, in addition to the rest of the formula. When more is known about the PRECISE chemical defects in aging, I shall of course do just this.

Needless to say I am well aware of the many factors modifying enzyme activity and synthesis, and take these broadly into account when I use the word homeostatic in describing the ensuing enzyme synthesis. At times, it may be necessary to invoke these factors, as well, especially in future work that I can foresee.

I believe that the preceding pages should provide some account of the present "state of the art" as far as "RNA therapy" is concerned, and provide a good basis for knowing what is possible right now, in the present or near present with the actual therapy of aging. I do not consider that other approaches are as malleable or as effective, though for example, much that they describe, as in the work of Harmon or others who preceded him, or in the work of Bjorksten, in respect of their anti-oxidant and protein linkage theories, respectively, is correct in its observations. It does not seem likely that aging, whether it begins in the DNA or affects the DNA by way of lysosomes or nitochondria, has one simple cause or mechanism of causation.

While it may be useful to take these causes into account, therapy must look toward the repair of the damage involved at the points or places of involvement, and it is here that nucleic acid containing repair systems must be primarily involved. I believe I have also amply shown the vast importance of a diet richer in nucleic acids in the prevention or retardation of aging, and the converse, of a diet poor in nucleic acids as being distinctly involved in the causation of aging. I have no yet invoked a set of chemical reactions in the precise causation of aging. It is of course probable that nucleic acids or derivatives are involved in just such a set of reactions, and that antioxidants may involve one or some of these reactions. As you know, I have demonstrated the antianoxia effect of nucleic acids, i.e., their use in increasing the efficiency of the utilization of ozygen, and perhaps oxidation more broadly conceived. It is entirely conceivable that free radical and other formations involving a helterskelter form of oxidation occur less readily in a body given optimal nourishment and optimal amounts of nucleic acids in the diet, and that damage thus occuring, is much more readily repaired. The same applies to cross linking. At this point I can only assume that this is so, until this can be experimentally demonstrated. The increased adaptability of the organism, i.e., cells, in the animals or humans given nucleic acids make this a good possibility, even a probability.

As you know, there is much indirect evidence for the existence of a so-called "biologic clock", that seems to limit the life span of species and possibly members of a given species. Its place, nature and mode of operation are unknown, but it would appear to operate in some primarily catabolic way. When more is known here, this too will be controlled in much more punctate ways. In the meantime, the nucleic acid containing (directed) metabolic system appears to offer the best hope of repairing the increasing damage this unknown process causes.

Important for those in the present to retard aging, is to increase the quantity of nucleic acids in the diet or to have a physician treat them with maximum tolerated doses of nucleic acids, as well as a broad spectrum of vitamins, minerals and trace minerals and an associated diet containing sufficient high quality protein and certain unsaturated fatty acids. Nucleic acids in the diet can be gotten from extra fish, sea food, nuts, as well as from many health foods. Extra fluids including water, fruit and vegetable juices and a glass or two of milk, all totalling at least 8–10 or so glasses, daily, depending on intake, should be taken with a diet rich in nucleic acids. Proper advice here can only be gotten by guidance from a knowledgeable physician, and I advise this in all cases.

Additionally, I look forward to the hopefully near future when the enzyme uricase or an active fragment can be taken, to increase very much the tolerated doses of nucleic acids. This alone would increase life expectancy markedly to double or triple the present life span, if experience in animals and man is any indication here. There are certain ways, obviously, to accomplish this. Apart from finding a relatively stable, active, nonantigenic fragment, it may be possible to inject a virus non-damaging, with this enzyme. As you know, apes, man and the Dalmation dog do not have this enzyme. Why this lack is unknown, and for man this has been a most costly evolutionary step. Perhaps some presently unknown advantage was gained, but from my point of view this is probably one important way our creator has to how limited our life spans. It appears that it is of utmost importance to pursue work on this enzyme in the above sense.

Another matter of importance is shown by my development of a skin cream, containing, among other things nucleic acid related components which are the primary source of its antiaging, antiwrinkle and skin lightening actions on the human skin. I believe this is the first obvious and clearly visible direct antiaging action of nucleic acids, or rather, a nucleic acid-containing system, on human beings. The cream also has a marked action in many degenerative skin conditions, as acne, psoriasis, burns, abraded skin and keloids which it shrinks rapidly. This activity demonstrates the basic antiaging power of a nucleic acid-containing system, and because it would in modified form be injectable would probably do the same for the body as a whole, where concentrations actually present in the cells might be made higher. As mentioned, this is presently the path I am pursuing.

The preceding should summarize my present outlook on aging and what can be done in the present or near present. I believe this work clearly shows that it is possible today to avoid the main thrust of aging and even to stay young.

Professor D. F. Chebotarev, director of the Russian Institute of Gerontology in Kiev has recently published a book on aging for the average reader and I am very grateful that he responded when I asked him for the Russian point of view. Very much abbreviated, his thoughts on aging and advice he gives in his book are as follows:

He feels that not only genetic factors influence aging but that many other factors play an important role in the aging process. Some of them are the way of life, profession, intensity of work, diet, organization of rest periods, environment, climate and past illnesses and diseases. He notes that our brain and muscle age least when used most. (I believe that this is one of the major points many researchers agree on. It is therefore good advice to stay physically and mentally active). He also agrees that as of today we have a few good indications of what aging is but we don't really know exactly what causes it. Since we don't know yet how to prevent aging we should also make studies on how to make old age more comfortable for the elderly. One of the main functions of clinics dealing with aging people should be to advise people what to expect and how to adjust to changes which come with age. Older people should not be separated from the rest of society and they should continue as long as possible in their professions. Based on observations of elderly people, it has become obvious that many times psychological factors are far more important than the actual state of the organism.

Very important in preventing aging is the ability to live a rational life, preserving normal activity of the nervous system, the heart and circulatory system and other systems which regulate the exchange of materials within the body.

WAY OF LIFE: USEFUL ACTIVITY PLUS PROPER DIET PLUS ACTIVE REST.

The factors that are important for staying young and healthy for a longer period of time are: CORRECTLY ORGANIZED WORK ACTIVITY AND REST PERIODS plus PROPER DIET plus ACTIVE EXERCISE plus PLEASANT INTERPERSONAL RELATIONSHIP WITH PEOPLE. These factors influence the nervous and endocrine systems in a positive way, thus aiding the system to sustain balance.

Machmud Ejvanson who reached the age of 150 states that his secret to long life was his everyday work. He can not imagine his life without work and without a goal—not strenuous work, but work which is combined with reasonable rest periods. Older people should perhaps remain in their professions as long as possible, but the load should obviously be lighter. A study of 500 men was conducted in Moscow. These men were in professions which had little physical activity and it was shown that they had very high incidents of arteriosclerosis and other diseases of the heart and circulatory system. A good exercise program together with the right rest periods and a well planned life is of the greatest importance.

A good diet also carries a high priority. Proteins are very important. As we get older we should make sure that we limit our carbohydrate and fat intake and older people should eat some foods low in cholesterol. He points out the life shortening effect of obesity.

Exercise is not only physical work but also what he terms active rest like fun exercise: skiing, skating, swimming etc. Studies at the Institute in Kiev have shown that physical activity, especially for elderly persons, is exremely useful. One of the most important reasons for aging is lack of activity of the muscular system. Activity acts positively on the central nervous system, and improves working ability of cells of the nervous system. Heart-circulatory system, heart muscles, blood pressure and lower incidence of arteriosclerosis are also influenced by exercise.

PREVENTIVE MEASURES discussed by Professor Chebotarev are:

Vitamin therapy: Very useful. Recent studies have shown that older people generally have vitamin deficiencies. The B-vitamins, vitamins C and E are very important. Vitamin combinations have been used with great success.

Novocaine: has successfully been used in a number of internal diseases, in surgical cases and illnesses due to changes in the nervous system. It is a necessary ingredient for life, it acts on hormones.

Endocrine therapy: should be used in conjunction with other treatments. Hormonal therapy should be used with care.

Cell therapy: All possibilities of cell therapy have not as yet been explored. But positive results have been seen to take place on the nervous system and endocrine system.

The fight for a long and healthy life is in fact a fight against premature aging and illness.

Hans Selye, Professor of medicine at the University of Montreal, is the internationally accepted authority on stress. He has discovered many of the basic facts about stress and later actually identified many hormones that play an important role in the biochemistry of stress. Since stress is such an important area, I contacted Professor Selye and discussed a few points with him. Since he is very busy and is also writing a new book (*Earn Thy Neighbors' Love*, which is a biologically founded code of conduct of life), he was not able to contribute a short article on stress, but allowed me to quote him extensively from his book *The Stress of Life*.* Talking about this book he says:

The main purpose of this book is to tell, in a generally understandable language, what medicine has learned about stress.

No one can live without experiencing some degree of stress all the time. You may think that only serious

---

The Stress of Life, McGraw-Hill Book Company, New York, 1956. Quoted by permission of the publisher.

disease or intensive physical or mental injury can cause stress. This is false. Crossing a busy intersection, exposure to a draft or even sheer joy are enough to activate the body's stress-mechanism to some extent. Stress is not even necessarily bad for you; it is also the spice of life, for any emotion, any activity causes stress. But, of course, your system must be prepared to take it. The same stress which makes one person sick can be an invigorating experience for another.

It is through the *general adaptation syndrome,* or G.A.S. (the main subject of this book), that our various internal organs—especially the endocrine glands and the nervous system—help to adjust us to the constant changes which occur in and around us.

Life is largely a process of adaptation to the circumstances in which we exist. A perennial give-and-take has been going on between living matter and its inanimate surroundings, between one living being and another, ever since the dawn of life in the prehistoric oceans. The secret of health and happiness lies in successful adjustment to the ever-changing conditions on this globe; the penalties for failure in this great process of adaptation are disease and unhappiness. The evolution through endless centuries from the simplest forms of life to complex human beings was the greatest adaptive adventure on earth. The realization of this has fundamentally influenced our thinking, but there is not much we can do about it. Here we are, such as we are; and whether or not man is pleased with the result, he cannot change his own inherited structure.

But there is another type of evolution which takes place in every person during his own lifetime from birth to death: this is adaptation to the stresses and strains of everyday existence. Through the constant interplay between his mental and bodily reactions, man has it in his power to influence this second type of evolution to a considerable extent, especially if he understands its mechanism and has enough will power to act according to the dictates of human intellect.

Stress is essentially the rate of all the wear and tear caused by life. It will take a whole book to explain the complex mechanisms through which the body can reduce this type of wear and tear. But let me say here, by way of an introduction, that although we cannot avoid stress as long as we live, we can learn a great deal about how to keep its damaging side-effects to a minimum. For instance, we are just beginning to see that many common diseases are largely due to errors in our adaptive response to stress, rather than to direct damage by germs, poisons, or other external agents. In this sense many nervous and emotional disturbances, high blood pressure, gastric and duodenal ulcers, certain types of rheumatic, allergic cardiovascular, and renal diseases appear to be essentially *diseases of adaptation.*

In view of all this, stress is undoubtedly an important personal problem for everybody. So much has been written for the general public about my work on stress by others, that I gradually came to feel the need of telling the story in my own words. Writing this book certainly helped me. I hope it will also help you. It helped me because I have spent the last twenty years doing experiments on stress and thinking about their interpretations. I have written six large volumes and several hundred scientific articles about stress in technical journals for specialists. But this is the first chance I have had to put the really salient points together and get a bird's-eye view, not only of the facts discovered in the laboratory, but also of the thoughts and emotions inspired by constant pre-occupation with the nature of stress in health and disease. The urge to share with others the thrill of adventure which comes from penetrating, even if ever so slighly, into hitherto unknown depths of life can become a major source of

205

stress in itself. I just had to get this book out of my system, and doing so has certainly helped me.

In a similar sense, I hope this account will help my readers—physicians and laymen alike—who do not have an opportunity of experiencing at first hand all those manifold satisfactions which come from design-ing experimental plans and acquiring the techniques necessary to solve some of those problems of life which concern us all.

But I should like to think that this book may offer an even more practical kind of help. Psychoanalysis has shown that knowledge about oneself has a cura-tive value. I think this is also true of psychosomatic, and perhaps even of what we call purely somatic, or bodily, derangements. The struggle for understanding is one of the most characteristic features of our spe-cies; that is why man is called *Homo sapiens*. The sat-isfaction of this urge is our destiny.

But what does Professor Selye think about the maxi-mum possible life span? I'll quote him again:

What makes me so certain that the natural human life-span is far in excess of the actual one is this:

Among all my autopsies (and I have performed quite a few), I have never seen a man who died of old age. In fact, *I do not think anyone has ever died of old age yet.* To permit this would be the ideal accomplishment of medical research (if we disregard the unlikely event of someone discovering how to re-generate adaptation energy). To die of old age would mean that all the organs of the body would be worn out proportionately, merely by having been used too long. This is never the case. We invariably die because one vital part has worn out too early in proportion to the rest of the body. Life, the biologic chain that holds our parts together, is only as strong as its weakest vital link. When this breaks—no matter which vital link it be—our parts can no longer be held together as a single living being.

You will note I did not say "our parts die," because this is not necessarily so. In tissue cultures, isolated cells of a man can go on living for a long time after he, as a whole, has died. It is only the complex organization of all our cells into a single individual that necessarily dies when one vital part breaks down. An old man may die because one worn-out, hardened artery breaks in his brain, or because his kidneys can no longer wash out the metabolic wastes from his blood, or because his heart muscle is damaged by excessive work. But *there is always one part which wears out first and wrecks the whole human machinery*, merely because the other parts cannot function without it.

Dr. Selye has discovered that our body has two defense systems against stress; the adrenal gland supplies hormones for both of them. One group he calls syntoxic hormones which work as tranquilizers to prevent harmful effects of relatively minor stresses. The other group of hormones he calls catatoxic hormones that help in the destruction of toxic materials. If he could find ways to activate them, we might even get some more help against cancer from these hormones.

On implications and applications Professor Selye says:

The most important *applications of the stress concept as regards purely somatic medicine* are derived from the discovery that the body can meet various aggressions with the same adaptive-defensive mechanism. A dissection of this reaction teaches us how to combat disease by strengthening the body's own defenses against stress.

This also has important *psychosomatic implications*. Bodily changes during stress act upon mentality and vice versa. Only by dissecting our troubles can we clearly distinguish the part played by the stressor from that of our own adaptive measures of defense and surrender. We shall see how this helps us to handle ourselves during the stress of everyday life, and in particular, how to tune down when we are wrought up, how to overcome insomnia, and how to get out of certain grooves of stereotyped behavior.

Stress research also has far-reaching *philosophic implications*. We shall see that stress plays a role in such diverse manifestations of life as aging, the development of individuality, the need for self-expression, and the formulation of man's ultimate aims. Stress is usually the outcome of a struggle for the self-preservation (the homeostasis) of parts within a whole. This is true of individual cells within man, of man within society, and of individual species within the whole animate world. After surveying the emotions which govern interpersonal relations (the thirst for approval, the terror of censure, the feelings of love, hate, gratitude, and revenge), we come to the conclusion that the incitement, by our actions, of gratitude in others is most likely to assure our safety within society. Why not seek this consciously as a long-range aim in life? No other philosophy has the exquisite property of necessarily transforming all our natural, egotistic impulses into altruism without curtailing any of their self-protecting value.

But man cannot think only of future safety; he wants more immediate rewards; he has a need for self-expression; he wants to enjoy the pleasures his senses can bring; he wants the satisfaction and equanimity which come from reverently contemplating the great wonders of Creation. In the light of research on stress, my advice would be:

> Fight always for the highest attainable aim
> But never put up resistance in vain.

There is no ready-made success formula which will suit everybody. We are all different. But, since man is essentially a rational being, the better he knows what makes him tick, the more likely he will be to make a success of life. Man's ultimate aim is to express himself as fully as possible, according to his own lights.

The most important lesson we can learn from Dr. Selye's work is that we have to know ourselves well enough so that we know when a stress situation arises, if we can adapt to it or if we should rather take evasive action and flee the problem.

In his book Professor Selye talks about many other interesting topics like "Stress in a nutshell, "The nature of adaptation," "The diseases of adaptation," "On being keyed up," "How to tune down" and many others. The book is available as an inexpensive paperback and is on my list of highly recommended books.

CHAPTER 20

Check Yourself

How high is your risk of aging prematurely?
and
What is your chance of slowing down your aging process?

CHECK YOURSELF. What is your chance of slowing down the aging process?

Aging is an extremely complex process; many different factors can affect it. In order of decreasing priorities, only factors are listed that have been shown to increase or decrease the average life expectancy of humans or test animals, or that can improve the general health or mental alertness, or for which we have good indications that they should slow down the aging process in accord with existing theories on aging.

Large doses of vitamins or other compounds are only mentioned when there is no evidence from research results that they could do damage whenever taken in the right amounts.

Instructions for checking yourself:

a) Read column A.
b) I hope you have read the entire book; if not, read up on the material in the corresponding chapters or references listed in column B before you assign any points for your answer.
c) Enter the correct number of points in column C.

1) Nutrition:
    4 pts. for following the rules on "super-nutrition."
    2 pts. for knowing a little about good nutrition and sometimes following them.
    no pts.: doesn't know any basic facts about nutrition.

Ch. 4
also: A. Davis: *Let's Eat Right To Keep Fit.*
    R. Williams, *Nutrition Against Disease.*

2) Diets:
    3 pts. for "super-nutrition" diets.
    1 pt.: reduces the number of calories only.
    no pts. for the "Stillman protein and lots of water only" diet, the "carbohydrate only diet" or other idiocies.

Ch. 4

3) Smoking:
    6 pts. for not smoking.
    2 pts.: less than 10 cigarettes/day.
    no pts.: more than 10 cigarettes/day.

Ch. 15

4) Exercise I
    3 pts. for following a planned exercise program.
    1 pt. for sometimes trying.
    no pts.: has no exercise program.

Ch. 16

5) Exercise II: When you exercise
    3 pts. for doing several different types of exercise including jogging.
    1 pt. for doing one specific exercise only.
    no pts.: no exercise.

Ch. 16

6) Stress I: work
    3 pts.: no stress, you can handle it.
    1 pt.: sometimes under stress, sometimes uptight.
    no pts.: often under stress, your job is liable to give you ulcers.

Ch. 7
Ch. 19

7) Stress II: your partner in love
    3 pts.: you look forward to being with him (her); you are relaxed

Ch. 7
Ch. 19

| | **A** | **B** | **C** |

and happy whenever you are together.

1 pt.: its not 100% but problems
are often ironed out easily.
no pts.: you fight a lot; he (she)
doesn't really turn you on any
more.

8) Stress III: your entire life: Ch. 7
   3 pts.: you are at peace with the   Ch. 19
   world and yourself.
   1 pt.: it could be much better,
   but such is life.
   no pts.: you are not happy at all
   with what you do and are.

9) Your brain:
   3 pts.: you exercise your brain,   Ch. 4
   keep mentally alert, read a lot,   Ch. 8
   think a lot, new ideas are exciting. Ch. 19
   1 pt.: due to other circumstances
   you don't have the time to exercise your brain enough, sometimes active.
   no pts.: think—lazy, your major
   brain exercise is to watch TV.

10) Overweight: Ch. 4
    4 pts.: normal weight, not flabby.   Ch. 17
    2 pts.: 5 to 10% overweight.   Ch. 19
    no pts.: more than 10% over-
    weight.

11) Multi-vitamins with minerals.   Ch. 4
    3 pts.: take 1 to 2 per day.
    1 pt.: take it only sometimes or
    take vitamin without minerals.
    no pts.: don't take any.

12) Vitamin C.   Ch. 4
    3 pts.: takes lots of vitamin C.   Ch. 13, 15
    1 pt.: eats foods high in vita-
    min C.
    no pts.: don't take any or very
    little.

13) Vitamin A.   Ch. 4
    3 pts.: takes extra vitamin A.   Ch. 13

1 pt.: eats foods containing A.
no pts.: none of the two above.

14) B-Complex   Ch. 4
    3 pts. for taking a good B-com-
    plex

15) 2 pts. for taking some extra Nia-   Ch. 4
    cin amide   Ch. 15
    2 pts. for taking some extra pan-
    tothenic acid

16) Calcium and vitamin D.   Ch. 4
    3 pts.: takes bone meal and vit. D.
    1 pt.: eats foods high in calcium.
    no pts.: none of the above.

17) Vitamin E.   Ch. 4
    3 pts.: takes at least 200 mg.   Ch. 5
    extra vitamin E per day.   Ch. 6
    1 pt.: eats foods high in vita-   Ch. 13 and 19
    min E.
    no pts.: don't take any.

18) Sulfur amino acids.   Ch. 4
    3 pts.: takes sulfur amino acids   Ch. 5
    or foods high in sulfur amino   Ch. 13, 15 and 19
    acids.   Ch. 19
    1 pt.: takes sulfur amino acids
    containing foods only sometimes.
    no pts.: don't take any.

19) Nucleic acids.   Ch. 4, 11, 20
    3 pts.: planned nucleic acid cures
    or eats lots of foods containing
    nucleic acids like fish, caviar,
    yeast.
    1 pt.: gets nucleic acids just some-
    times, more or less by accident.
    no pts.: doesn't take any nucleic
    acids
    doesn't eat foods high in nucleic
    acids

20) Air pollution.   C. 18
    3 pts.: lives in clean air or has an
    air purifier installed in the home.
    1 pt.: live in medium polluted
    areas.
    no pt.: for living in N.Y. City,

	A	B	C

L.A., south side of Chicago or any other highly polluted area.

21) Alcohol.   Ch. 8
3 pts.: no alcohol or only from time to time.
1 pt.: only wine sometimes.
no pts.: regular drinker.

For the following you can give yourself 2 points each maximum:

22) Take wheat germ oil.   Ch. 5
                                         Ch. 20

23) Take brewer's yeast.   Ch. 4

24) Take lecithin or eat lecithin rich   Ch. 13
foods.

25) Don't eat before you go to bed   Ch. 4
but drink a glass of water before   Ch. 7
you go to sleep.

26) Drink multi-vegetable juices.   Ch. 4

27) Sleep in a cool room and get   Ch. 7
enough rest all the time.

28) Take some safflour oil or use it   Ch. 4
for cooking.

29) Take some magnesium and   Ch. 4
calcium (dolomite, etc.).

30) Education: BS, BA or higher

EVALUATION:

One through 10 carry an extremely high priority; they are the basic requirements for reaching a high age while staying physically fit and mentally alert. If you are seriously concerned, you should get very close to 35 points for these ten factors alone. If you are not close to 35 points remember that you can always do something about it; it never is too late (especially to quit smoking or at least to cut down).

NOW LET'S TAKE A LOOK AT THE TOTAL NUMBER OF POINTS:

0 to 15 points: Are you sure you are still alive ?????

Let's be serious now. Your main concern should be H-E-A-L-T-H. Do something about nutrition, exercise, smoking and stress first—then try again. 16 to 31 points: Face it, your risk factor is pretty high. You probably scored less than 20 points in the first 10 questions. That's where you have to start your improvements. Don't try to improve everything at once. If you don't smoke you have a good start; if you smoke, get a cancer check at first. Read a good book on health and nutrition and act accordingly. 32 to 46 points: You are on your way. Obviously you know a little about health and your trouble seems to be to stick to the rules. Minor improvements and a little more determination can make a really long-lived species out of you. 47 to 62 points: Good show, you obviously know what you are doing. Keep up the good work. Stay on top of everything by reading good health literature like *Prevention* magazine, etc. Make changes as logic dictates. 63 and up: It sounds too good to be true. Don't overdo it. Don't get nervous and distressed if you are on your way to work and suddenly remember that you forgot to take your vitamin pills. You are very well-informed about health and stick to the rules. You could try to do something about the health of your friends and neighbors; take them along to a health club or to a health food store and buy them a multi-vegetable juice.

Other possible methods of rejuvenation as outlined in Chapters 10, 11, and 14 were not included in the test you just completed.

And again a reminder: Please let your government representatives know how you feel about limiting the availability of food supplements to you (Re. Congressional Bill H.R. 2323, see last page in Chapter 4).

WE SOMETIMES HEAR THAT SCIENTISTS ARE LOOKING FOR "THE CAUSE OF AGING," HOW

DO WE KNOW THAT THERE IS ONLY ONE CAUSE? We don't. Human aging research is so complicated that it is almost impossible for a researcher to work in more than one area. Often they hope that they will find the answer. From what we know so far, aging is an extremely complicated process with many different causes.

MANY SCIENTISTS SEEM TO AGREE THAT "AGING IS A CONSTANT LOSS OF CELLS," DOESN'T THAT MEAN THAT THE PROBLEM IS SOLVED? No, because we don't really know all the causes for this constant loss of cells.

WHAT THEN ARE THE MAJOR CAUSES FOR THIS CELL LOSS? There are several and we don't really know which one is the most important. Some of them are stress in general, damage done to the DNA, the accumulation of large molecules in our body and the cell-damaging effect of what the chemist calls "free radicals."

IF THE CAUSES OF AGING ARE SO MANIFOLD, CAN WE REALLY DO SOMETHING ABOUT THEM? Yes. The correct precautionary actions can lengthen our average life span tremendously. Besides, scientists predict an average life span of about 170 years if we can solve and effectively counteract only 10% of the aging problem.

DOES DIETING AFFECT THE AGING PROCESS? Yes. A wrong diet can make you age at ten to fifteen times the normal rate. That means that if you diet the wrong way for one week, you could do as much damage to your system as 30 weeks of normal aging would do. Our cells are kept functioning normally by a fine balance of hundreds of chemical reactions. If we interfere with these reactions we do serious damage to our system; and that's exactly what happens if you go on one of these diets that limit you to one type of food only.

IF YOU ARE ON THE "STILLMAN PROTEIN AND LOTS OF WATER DIET" YOU REALLY LOSE A LOT OF WEIGHT. WHY IS THIS SO? Because you mess up the entire spectrum of chemical reactions in your system. At first you decrease the salt concentration in your body fluids by flushing it out with large quantities of water. Then you make it extremely difficult to maintain the acidity in your entire system constant since you form only a smaller number of chemicals in your oxidation reactions and since many of the compounds necessary to maintain a constant acidity are already flushed out. Your chance to get the essential fatty acids is almost zero and this is extremely important. If you are concerned about your long-term health this is certainly not the way to lose weight.

ROYAL JELLY IS SUPPOSED TO HAVE SOME REJUVENATING POWERS. IS THERE ANY TRUTH IN IT? Royal jelly is a bee product; it contains large quantities of pantothenic acid, a B vitamin. It is also found in smaller concentrations in honey. Professor R. Williams has extended the average life span of test animals by feeding them extra pantothenic acid. The importance of the B vitamins is well established.

DOES THE REMOVAL OF THE SEX ORGANS HAVE A REJUVENATING EFFECT? Many experiments on animals and humans claim a rejuvenating effect upon removal of the sex organs and glands. But what would be life without sex?

217

WHAT IS PANGAMIC ACID? It's a compound found in many seeds and brewers yeast, sometimes known as vitamin B-15. It seems to be an extremely important compound that can supply our cells with lots of oxygen. No harmful effects are known and it could be quite helpful in slowing down the aging process. But, you cannot buy it in the United States thanks to another decision of the Food and Drug Administration. Why? Heaven knows. Read more about it in *Prevention*, May 1968.

HOW CAN FASTING DELAY AGING? There are no data available that it works on humans. We know that animals can be made to live longer by underfeeding but this is not really fasting. According to the waste products theory on aging, toxic materials from processed foods and oxidation products collect in the cell because the removal is too slow. These toxic materials poison the cell and make it age faster. Fasting allows the body to rid itself of these toxic materials. This effect is good, but the complete lack of foods which your body needs at all times probably outweighs the good effects. Fasting might have a positive effect but you should do it only for a very short time period. I believe that you can achieve a better effect by not overeating, sleeping in a cool room and drinking an extra glass of water with every meal and before you go to sleep.

A NEWSPAPER REPORTED RECENTLY THAT A BRITISH DOCTOR RECOMMENDS ESTROGEN PILLS FOR OLDER PEOPLE IN ORDER TO LIVE A LONGER AND HEALTHIER LIFE. ISN'T ESTROGEN THE CHEMICAL IN BIRTH CONTROL PILLS? Yes. Estrogen makes the body hold water. This extra water puffs up the cells so that the skin of an older person might look a little younger. An increase of the body defenses also seems to be connected with estrogens. This might be a good reason for older women to stay on the pill but I can't see what it would do for a man, especially when I think about his sex life.

WHAT IS AEVIT-B15? Aevit is a combination of the vitamins A and E developed by a Russian Professor, Y. Shpirt, who used it successfully in the treatment of gangrene together with vitamin B-15. These compounds are used quite frequently in the treatment of atherosclerosis and coronary sclerosis in Russia.

WHY ARE ESSENTIAL FATTY ACIDS SO IMPORTANT? In order to understand this we have to explain the hormone-chain-of-command. Hormones modify rates of enzyme reactions in the cell. When a hormone brings a message to a cell, it is normally too big to pass through the cell membrane into the cell. It therefore passes the message at the cell wall to a compound called cyclic Adenosinemonophosphate (cAMP). This cAMP gets the message to the enzyme with the help of compounds called prostaglandins. And here we have the reason for the importance of essential fatty acids: prostaglandins are made from essential fatty acids. So, if you are lacking essential fatty acids, the modification of enzyme reactions in the cells is seriously hampered and biochemical reactions in the cells are messed up completely.

WHAT IS THE ACTION OF INSULIN IN THE BODY? There are several hormones in the body that control the glucose level in the blood. Somatotrophin regulates the conversion of glycogen into glucose and protein into glucose. Glucagon mobilizes sugar reserves and raises the blood sugar level. When you eat your pick-me-up candy bar the blood sugar level rises.

The blood sugar, however, cannot get into the cells to the mitochondria without somebody opening the door. Insulin is the door-opener that lets the glucose into the cell. It seems that overweight people have a very active insulin mechanism. That means as soon you eat sugar containing foods, the blood sugar goes up but decreases very rapidly because of the action of insulin. This decrease in blood sugar makes you hungry again. And more and more sugar is converted into fat.

MORE QUESTIONS AND ANSWERS

DR. D. DAVIES (NEW SCIENTIST, FEBRUARY 1, 1973) REPORTED ON A GROUP OF OLD PEOPLE LIVING IN VILCABAMBA, EQUADOR AND STATED THAT THEY SMOKE BETWEEN 40 TO 60 CIGARETTES AND DRINK TWO CUPS OF UNREFINED RUM PER DAY. HOW COME THESE PEOPLE CAN GET THAT OLD? These people really don't reach such old age as reported for the other areas on this earth where people get very old. While the Russians have a man who is 167, the oldest Vilcabamba is only 130 where records confirm this age. For example, out of 819 people there was only one woman in the age group 110 to 119 and only 3 men in the age group over 120. Many factors that contribute to a long life are also present: low calorie intake, physical fitness, good attitude toward life. The cigarettes are home-made and we don't really know the composition of their "tobacco." The village of Vilcabamba is about 5000 feet above sea level. At such a high altitude alcohol has a much higher vapor pressure than at sea level. The amount of alcohol that a person exhales through his lungs (you can smell alcohol in the breath of a person) will be much more at a higher altitude than at sea level. So, a large percentage of alcohol evaporates before it can do any harm.

WHAT IS THE LONGEVITY QUOTIENT? The LQ is frequently used by E. Palmore who has published several interesting articles in the "Gerontologist". Dr. Palmore studied large groups of older people and found that among others, work satisfaction, happiness rating, physical functioning and tobacco use were the four strongest predictors of longevity when age, sex, and race are controlled by the Longevity Quotient. The Longevity Quotient is the observed number of years survived after an initial interview divided by the actuarially expected number of years. An LQ of 1.0 means that the person survived exactly as long as expected and an LQ of 1.5 means that the person survived 50% longer than expected. An LQ of 0.50 means that the person survived only half as long as expected. Some interesting LQ's showed the effect of education on longevity. The LQ's were for a Ph.D. 1.23, BA 1.10, high school 1.0 and less than 3 years of elementary school 0.82. Dr. Palmore also stated that mobility accounts for more of the variance in longevity than any other single predictor.

ARE THERE ANY WELL KNOWN DOCTORS THAT CRITICIZE THE AMA? Yes, lots of doctors don't agree with the AMA. Take for example Dr. John Knowles who at the age of 35 was appointed General Director of the Massachusetts General Hospital in Boston and who at the age of 47 became president of the billion dollar Rockefeller foundation. When Dr. Knowles was nominated by Robert Finch for an important HEW post, the AMA lobby let the Government know that they didn't want him in such an important position. Why? Maybe some of Dr. Knowles' ideas will give us the answer: Dr. Knowles feels that many surgeons are performing unnecessary surgery, that American medicine is pretty bad, that doctors make too much money and that the free market favors high cost curative medicine rather than preventive medicine.

When asked what's the advantage of emphasizing expensive life saving techniques over simple prevention Dr. Knowles answered:

"For three obvious reasons: First, acute curative medicine is more interesting intellectually. Two, it's more gratifying emotionally. Try telling someone 40 years old to stop smoking, lose weight, get regular exercise, come back in six months and then send him a bill for $30. The consumer will have none of this either because he has no evidence you've done anything for him. It takes two to tango. Three, it's much more rewarding financially to treat a man for an acute coronary for three weeks than it is to see him for an hour once a year to prevent the coronary." (157).

WHY DOES THE AMA FAVOR SUCH HIGH COST CURATIVE OVER PREVENTIVE MEDICINE? We don't really know, but the $10 million interest of the AMA retirement fund in the drug industry might give us a hint there. I would define this as a sincere conflict of interest. A ruling of the AMA states that it would be questionable ethics for a physician to invest in drug companies. The little guy can't do it, but the boss can!

Appendix

Organic Foods

My last comments in this book will air my views on organic foods. There have been so many incorrect statements made about these foods that, though they neither aid nor hinder the aging processes, I would like to clear up a few facts while we're on the subject of nutrition.

Please don't mistake organic foods for natural foods.

Organic foods are supposedly grown on land which is not treated with pesticide. Only natural fertilizers such as manure are used. Weeding is done mechanically or by hand. The processing of organic foods is done without chemicals, flour and sugar are not bleached and no preservatives are added. Milk and meat are obtained from animals that are fed only natural nutrients and that graze on pastures that are not treated with chemicals or pesticides.

The basic idea of organic foods is "back to nature" and away from chemicals and pesticides. That sounds good, but its rather like an advertisement for a bad product. The commercial sounds terrific but let's examine the product.

The basic nutrients that plants need (nitrogen, phosphorus and potassium) are absorbed from the ground by the plants in a salt form. These salts are the same in both manure and industrial fertilizers. But there are some other differences.

Manure contains a fixed ratio of these three nutrients while in industrial fertilizers these nutrients can be mixed in different ratios to be adapted to the soil's needs.

Industrial fertilizers do not contain the salts of the three nutrients in any poisonous form, they are less expensive and the yield per acre is higher with their use.

Natural fertilizers contain a lot of bulk that is good for only one type of soil.

Manures contain an extremely large number of bacteria and viruses. Organic food fanatics often advocate the use of human waste as fertilizer. This is still done in some countries (e.g. Japan and some poor European countries). Tourists cannot eat this food uncooked without getting ill; only native people have built up a resistance against these high bacteria and virus levels.

When pesticides are not used, more disease-carrying insects and their eggs are found on these foods. There is no government control over organic foods; but in my opinion, certain organic foods should carry a label: "Caution, the high level of bacteria and viruses on these foods can be hazardous to your health."

To use no preservatives in processing food is basically a good idea, but these preservatives prevent decomposition and the growth of bacteria and viruses. Besides, these preservatives are in foods only in very small quantities. We can decrease these quantities even further by eating fresh fruits and vegetables whenever possible. This may sound strange, but the preservative butylated hydroxytoluene, which we have been adding to our foods for a long time, is a chemical that can slow down the aging process. This preservative might be one of the constituents in youth drugs.

The pesticide problem was called to our attention by R. Carson in the book *Silent Spring*. The warnings about pesticides made a lot of sense at that time. It was not unusual then for farmers to use the wrong pesticides in unusually high quantities to make sure that they would get a good yield from their crops.

Since then, the government has tightened the regulations for the use of pesticides tremendously and with the sensible use of pesticides assured, our health should not be affected by these chemicals.

If you're worried about the pesticide that is still on the food when you buy it, please follow me through a little math:

Just after the plants have come out of the soil, two pounds (900 grams) of pesticide are applied per acre. There are about 25,000 plants on one acre. At the time of application, about 1/30 of the surface is covered by plants. The amount of atrazine (a pesticide) that reaches the plants is 30 grams. (900 ÷ 30 = 30 grams) Atrazine that reaches one plant is 1.2 mg. (30 ÷ 25,000 = 1.2) One mg is 1/1000g. Within four months at least 50% of the atrazine is broken down into harmless compounds. Fifty percent of 1.2 mg is 0.6 mg. If we consider corn, we eat only about 1/20 of this plant. (0.6 ÷ 20 = 0.03 mg.) A more reasonable number would be about *0.001 mg.* because we have not included in this calculation the breakdown of atrazine in the plant. In fact, the pesticide can even be blown away by wind and washed away by rain. The acute oral toxicity for atrazine for a person weighing 140 lbs. is expressed as LD 50 and is approximately 210,000 mg. This must be taken at one time. So, how many cobs of corn would you have to eat at one time to reach even 1/100 of the LD 50? About 60,000.

Two interesting reports might stimulate your thinking about this matter. Almost a year ago, R. Loible, a pest-control executive, and his wife were taking (over a 93-day period) ten milligrams of DDT every day—more than the average person would take in over a period of 80 years. So far they have not been affected at all (75). A real problem, however, consists of the fact that some pesticides accumulate in our system. We don't know anything about the long-term effects of small quantities of pesticides in our body. Naturally the best thing would be if we could prevent the deposition of even small quantities of pesticides in our system. We hope to achieve this by using pesticides that are not very stable over a longer time period.

"DDT may inhibit at least one kind of cancer." This is the assumption E. Laws made after experimenting with mice who had been fed a DDT-containing diet (76).

I am not proposing that DDT is a cure for cancer, but as you can see, there is more than one side to every story.

There are several other points we have to consider if we want to evaluate the value of organic foods.

People that buy organic foods always insist that they taste better. A good point. I have tried these foods myself and found that the taste is somewhat different in a positive way.

The proteins we get from beef often contain some diethylstilbestrol, a female sex hormone which is fed to the animals in order to make them a little heavier. And when Adelle Davis says "Why there are any fertile males left in this country when all the beef is stuffed with female sex hormones I'll be damned if I know" she has a damned good point there.

But again, we know that many nutrition experts like A. Davis buy their foods in regular food stores.

I personally believe that the value of organic foods is somehow over-emphasized. If you worry about aging, there are several other areas that carry a much higher priority than organic foods. If you are willing to pay more for these foods and believe in them then go ahead and buy them.

Even if organic foods delivered what they promise, this still wouldn't mean that we are going in the right direction. These foods with a limited volume and a raised price could only supply foods for a limited number of people. We have to find other ways to improve the quality of foods. The demand is there and food producers already react to it.

Take a walk through a modern supermarket and look around. What a collection of worthless filler materials, shelves full of sweets that don't have much nutritional value, bread made from white bleached flour, canned foods containing preservatives, sweet soda etc. etc. etc. If you know a little about foods you will recognize that 60 to 80% is junk and should be thrown out or fed to your enemies but you will also find some good foods. If you don't buy the worthless foods, then your store manager will not order them and since he wants to keep you as a customer, he will order what YOU want to buy.

REFERENCES

1. Personal communication with R. Passwater who is a consultant in gerontology at American Gerontological Laboratories, Inc.

2. American Gerontological Laboratories, Inc., Silver Springs, Md.
Schwarzhaupt KG, Cologne, Germany.
Bjorksten Research Laboratory, Madison, Wisconsin.
Cytobiologische Laboratorien GMBH, Heidelberg, Germany. And others.

3. L. Hayflick, "Human Cells and Aging," *Scientific American*, 218 (1968).

4. H. Selye and P. Prioreschi, "Stress Theory of Aging," N.W. Shock, Aging, some social and biological aspects. AAAS, 1960.

5. D. Harman, *Free Radical Theory of Aging*, J. Geront., 11, 298 (1956).

6. L. Szilard, *On the Nature of the Aging Process*, Proc. Natl. Acad. Sci., 45, 30 (1959).

7. C. Ponnamperuma, NASA, meeting of the New York Acad. of Sciences, 1971.

8. For a summary of vitamins see any latest edition of a good biochemistry textbook.

9. W. Kaufman, MD, physician in Connecticut.

10. I. Stone, biochemist, the man who got Linus Pauling interested in vitamin C (Carl Neuberg Medal Award dinner, New York, 1966).

11. R. Mumma, Pennsylvania State University, meeting of the Federation of American Societies for Experimental Biology, Chicago, 1971.

12. F. Klenner and F. Bartz, "The Key to Good Health: vitamin C, 1969.

13. R. Williams, *Biochemical Individuality*, Wiley, 1956.

14. L. Buch, R. Halpern, R. Smith, D. Streeter, L. Simon and M. Stout, Chem. & Eng. News, Febr. 14, 1972.

15. W. Bollag and F. Ott, "Vitamin A Säure in der

Tumortherapie," Schweiz. med. Wschr., 101, 17 (1971).

16. H. and D. Gershon, Israel Institute of Technology, Nature, 227, 1214 (1970).

17. R. Passwater and P. Welker, "Human Aging Research," American Laboratory, May 1971.

18. H. Eyring, Utah University press release August 31, 1971.

19. W. Pryor, "Radical Pathology," Chem. & Eng. News, June 7, 1971.

20. D. Harman, J. Geront., 12, 257 (1957).

21. J. Bjorksten, "The Cross Linkage Theory of Aging," J. of the Amer. Geriatr. Soc. 16, 408 (1968).

22. H. Staudinger, "Zur Entwicklung der Chemie der Hochpolymeren," Verlag Chemie, Germany, 1937.

23. J. Bjorksten, J. mer. Geriat. Soc., 8, 632 (1960).

24. J. Bjorksten, Finska Kemists Medd., 71, 69 (1962).

25. F. Verzar, Scientific American, 208, 110 (1963).

26. J. Bjorksten, J. Amer. Geriat. Soc., 13, 94 (1965).

27. A. Bailey, C. Peach and L. Fowler, J. Biochem., 117, 819 (1970).

28. R. Passwater, Chem. & Eng. News, in press.

29. L. Orgel, Proc. Natl. Acad. of Sciences.

30. A. Comfort, "The Biology of Senescence," Rinehart & Co. 1956.

31. G. Failla, Ann. N.Y. Acad. Sci., 17, 1124 (1958).

32. L. Szilard, Proc. Natl. Acad. Sci. 45, 30 (1959).

33. H.J. Curtis, "Das Altern, die biologischen Vorgänge," Jena, VEB Gustav Fischer, 1968.

34. H. Rhase, Scientific American, 223, 75 (1970).

35. D. Carpenter, Bull. of Math. Biophys. 487 (1969).

36. R. Walford, "The Immunologic Theory of Aging," Gerontologist, 4, 195 (1964).

37. J. Still, "A Cybernetic Theory of Aging," Med. Ann. Distr. Columbia, 25, 199 (1964).

38. R. Pearl, *The Rate of Living*, A. Knopf, 1928.

39. J. Hart and D. Carpenter, "Toward an Integrated Theory of Aging," American Laboratory, April 1971.

40. R. Passwater and P. Welker, "Human Aging Research," American Laboratory, April 1971.

41. C. Leake, Geriatrics, p. 97, March 1968.

42. C. Leake, Geriatrics, p. 100, February 1968.

43. W. Alvarez, Geriatrics, p. 65, September 1971.

44. H. De Vries, Geriatrics, p. 102, April 1971.

45. Personal communication with members of the National Clearinghouse for Smoking and Health.

46. P. Stephan, "The Secret of Eternal Youth," Arco, 1971.

47. P. Niehans, "Einführung in die Zellular-Therapie," 1959.

48. K. Grissinger, "Das Wunder der Frischzelle," 1961.

49. D. Whittingham, Nature, 233, September 10, 1971.

50. R. Wissler, University of Chicago, meeting of the Amer. Heart Association in Anaheim, Calif., 1971.

51. R. Mumma, meeting of the Federation of Amer. Societies for Experimental Biology, 1971.

52. B. Grossman, J. Cifonelli and A. Ozoa, "Inhibition of Atherosclerosis in Cholesterol-fed Rabbits by a Heparitin Sulfate," Atherosclerosis, 13, 103 (1971).

53. S. Gerö, "Therapie und Prävention der Atherosklerosis," Zeitschrift für Alternsforschung, 24, 301 (1971).

54. H. Bailey, "Vitamin E, Your Key to a Healthy Heart" Arco, 1964.

55. same as 2.

56. R. Walford, Symp. Soc. Exp. Biol., Acad. Press, 21, 351 (1967).

57. D. Bellamy, Exp. Geront. 3, 327 (1968).

58. K. Nandy and G. Bourne, Nature, London, 210, 313 (1966).

59. M. Földi, O. Zoltan and I. Gyori, Z. Geront. 3, 97 (1970).

60. T. Varkonyi, H. Domokos, M. Maurer, O. Zoltan, B. Csilik and M. Foldi, Z. Gerontol. 3, 254 (1970).

61. S. Friedman and C. Friedman, Nature, London, 200, 237 (1963).

62. S. Friedman, M. Nakashima and C. Friedman, Gerontologia, 11, 129 (1965).

63. G. Domagk and H. Zippel, Naturwissenschaften, 57, 152 (1970).

64. P. Gordon, S. Tobin, B. Doty and M. Nash, J. Geront., 23, 434 (1968).

65. B. Doty and P. Gordon, Fed. Proc., 54th Annual meeting, 1970.

66. K. Piez, Ann. Rev. Biochemistry, 37, 547 (1968).

67. R. Kohn and A. Leash, Exp. Molecular Path., 7, 354 (1967).

68. Personal communication with Dr. Bjorksten, 1972.

69. R. Pelton and R. Williams, Soc. Exp. Biol. Med., 99, 632 (1958).

70. R. Passwater, Chem. & Eng. News, October 1970.

71. Telephone conversation with R. Passwater on March 21, 1972.

72. L. Schneider, University of Arizona, Chem. and Eng. News, October 19, 1971.

73. B. Goldstein and H. Demopolous

74. W. Winkelstein and M. Gay, Univ. of Calif., Chem. & Eng. News, June 8, 1970, p. 45.

75. DDT eaters, Time, August 9, 1971.

76. E. Laws, Arch. Environ. Health, 23, 181 (1971).

77. P. Schmid and J. Stein, Ott Verlag Thoune, Switzerland. "Cell Research and Cellular Therapy."

78. L. Szilard, Proc. Natl. Acad. Sci., 45, 30 (1959).

79. A. Campbell, Lancet, 2, 1219 (1971).

80. A study on test animals by Dr. Velayudhan Nair at the Chicago Medical School has shown that LSD causes biochemical defects in their offspring. Chem. & Eng. News, September 7, 1970.

81. Report of the Inter-Society Commission for Heart Disease Resources. Chem. & Eng. News, December 21, 1970.

82. The Health Consequences of Smoking, U.S. Dept. of Health, Education and Welfare, 1971.

83. Average numbers for adult persons. The M.R.'s way depending on the age group in question.

84. J. Bjorksten, E. Weyer and S. Asham, FINSKA CHEMISTS. MEDD. 80, 4 (1971).

85. H. Daniell, Ann. Intern. Med., 75, 873 (1971).

86. L. Aurelian, J. Strandberg, L. Melendez and L. Johnson, Science, 174, 704 (1971).

87. S. Spiegelman, Science, 175, 182 (1972).

88. Dr. M. Baluda, University of Calif., Los Angeles Medical School. Chem. & Eng. News, Nov. 15, 1971, p. 79.

89. B.S. Frank, Nucleic Acid Therapy in Aging and Degenerative Disease, Psychological Library Publishers, 1968.

90. J. Amer. Med. Assoc., editorial, 209, 931 (1969).

91. B. W. Agranoff, Memory and Protein Synthesis, Scientific American, 216, 115 (1967).

92. R.J. Williams, How can the climate in medical education be changed?, Perspectives in Biology and Medicine, 14, 608 (1971).

93. Bill Barry, MIDWEST, Magazine of the Chicago Sun Times, February 6, 1972.

94. E. Ahrens, et al., Journal of Experimental Medicine, 90, 409, (1949).

95. H. Dyckerhoff, Die Biogenese der Proteine, Ärztl. Praxis 38, 1953 (1961).

96. E. Neumann and M. Grossmann: Effect of nucleic acid supplements in the diet on the rate of regeneration of rat liver: Amer. J. Physiol. 164, 251 (1951).

97. H. Hyden and E. Egyhazy: Glial RNA changes During a Learning Experiment in Rats, Proc. Natl. Acad. Sci., 49, 618 (1963).

98. D.E. Cameron: The use of Nucleic acid in Aged Patients with memory impairment, Amer. J. Psychiat. 114, 943 (1958).

99. M. Cachin, F. Pergola, J. De Brux, P. Brun: La Therapeutique par les Acides Ribonucleiques dans les Maladies du Foie, Presse Med. 56, 2612 (1961).

100. L. Cook, A. Davidson, D. Davis, H. Green, E. Fellows, Ribonucleic acid, Effect on Conditioned Behavior in Rats, Science 141, 268 (1963).

101. same as 100.

102. M. Bürger, Der Deoxyribonucleinsäure- und Ribonucleinsäuregehalt des Menschlichen Gehirns im Laufe des Lebens, Z. Altersforschung, 12, 133 (1958).

103. H. Hyden: Quantitative Assay of Compounds in Isolated, Fresh Nerve Cells and Glial Cells from Control and Stimulated Animals, Nature, 184, 433 (1959).

104. L. Polezhaev, S. Kolcin, G. Solnceva: Stimulation der Herzmuskelregeneration bei diptherischer Myocarditis, Berichte der Akademie der Wissenschaften der UDSSR, 164, (1965).

105. H. Dyckerhoff, Über die Synthese von Eiweiss im Organismus durch Ribonucleinsäuren, Die Medizinische, 25, 1029 (1958).

106. M. Wentz, Contribution à l'étude de la therapeutique geriatrique, Thèse, Fac. Med. Paris, 1962.

107. REGENERESEN nach Prof. Dr. H. Dyckerhoff, Laboratorium Prof. Dr. H. Dyckerhoff, Köln — Sülz, W—Germany.

108. Dr. David M. Spain, in cooperation with Dr. Henry Siegel and Dr. Victoria A. Bradess of New Yorks' Westchester County medical examiners office; Meeting of the American Heart Association, Dallas, 1972.

109. J. Gibson in "This Week Magazine," 7, 8, 1955.

110. R. Taylor, Hunza Health Secrets, Prentice Hall, 1964.

111. N. Solomon, "The Truth About Weight Control," page 167.

112. United Medical Laboratories, Lab News, December 1971.

113. Alcohol

114. M. Wilhelm, Family Circle, October 1971.

115. R. Passwater, Dietary Cholesterol, American Laboratory, Sept. 1972.

116. C. Spittle, Lancet, Dec. 11, 1971, p. 1280.

117. L. Dotti and coworkers, Newsweek, Sept. 11, 1950.

118. T. Blaine, Prevention, August 1972.

119. P. Lachance, R. Amer, FASEB, Atlantic City, Abstract 2882.

120. Personal communication with Prof. S. Needleman, Roosevelt Univ., Chicago.

121. R.J. Shamberger, J. Natl. Cancer Inst. 44: 931-936, 1970.

122. R.J. Shamberger, G. Rudolph, Experentia, 22: 116, 1966. Also: J. Natl. Cancer Inst.: 48: 1491-1499, 1972.

123. W. Jaffe, Exp. Med. Surg. 4: 278-282, 1946.

124. S. Haber, R. Wissler, Proc. Soc. Exp. Biol. Med. 111: 774-775, 1962.

125. R. Shamberger, S. Tytko, C. Willis, Cleveland Clinic Quarterly, Vol. 39, No. 3, p. 119-124.

126. Schwarzhaupt, Köln, W—Germany.

127. G. Brüning, Arztliche Praxis, 22, 4064, 1970.

128. E. Pakesch, Wiener Klinische Wochenscrift, 82, 211, 1970.

129. H. Marx, Fortschritte der Medizin, 79, 399, 1961.

130. A. Mock, Aerztliche Praxis, 22, 1999, 1970.

131. Robinson et al., Lancet, Febr. 5, 290, 1972.

132. J. P. Hrachovec, Fed. Proc., 31, 604, 1972.

133. Annual Meeting of the Gerontological Society, Dec. 1972, San Juan.

134. M. A. Nelson, Geriatrics, p. 103, Dec. 1972.

135. H. J. Curtis, The Gerontologist, Vol. 6, No. 3, p. 143, 1966.

136. H. J. Curtis, J. Leith, J. Tilley, J. Geront., 21: 268, 1966.

137. H. J. Curtis, Radiation Induced Cancer, Vienna, International Atomic Energy Agency, 1969.

138. H. J. Curtis, Radiation Research, 34: 315, 1968.

139. A. M. Nelson, Geriatrics, December 1972, p. 103.

140. N. Fabris, W. Pierpaoli, E. Sorkin, Nature, Dec. 29, 1972, p. 558.

141. B. Strehler, R. Johnson: Nature, Vol. 240, Dec. 15, 1972. p. 414.

142. H. J. Curtis et al., Meeting of the Gerontological
143. Society, Dec. 1972, San Juan.

144. H. J. Curtis, J. Tilley, J. of Gerontology, 1-7, 26, 1971.

145. L. Franks, Exper. Gerontology, 281-289, 5, 1970.

146. B. Strehler in H.W. Woolhouse, Aspects of the Biology of Aging, Cambridge University Press, 1967.

147 J. D. Wallace, D. H. Driscoll, C. G. Kalaminis, A. Neaves, J. M. Keever, K. Mc Nichols, U.S.P.H.S. Contract PH-86-67-291. Report, 1969.

148. R. A. Passwater, Cancer, New Directions, American Laboratory, June 1973.

149. W. S. Rickert and W. F. Forbes, Annual Meeting of the Gerontological Society, December, 1972. San Juan.

150. A. Goldstein, 57th annual meeting of the Federation of American Societies for Experimental Biology.

151. J.V.G.A. Durnin, O. G. Edholm, D. S. Miller, J. C. Waterlow, NATURE, 418, vol. 242, April 6, 1973.

152. Medical World News, Jan. 12, 1973.

153. National Geographic, January 1973.

154. "Chicago Today", October 2, 1972.

155. T. F. Berenstein, Zdravookhr. Beloruss. 18 (10), 34-36 (1972).

156. H. J. Sullivan, Geriatrics, March 1973.

157. P. Nobile, Chicago Sunday Sun-Times, "Midwest Magazine," May 27, 1973.

References quoted by Professor Hoepke (chapter 20)
Blumenberg Fr.W. in Zelltherapie 36 1969
                  in Stein Erfahrungen mit der Zelltherapie
                  Heidelberg Haug Verlag 1971
Bürger M. Die körperlichen Vorgänge beim Altern. Stuttgart 1958
Danchakoff V. Amer.J.Anat. 20 1916
Doms H. Altern,Tod und Verjüngung. Ergebn.d.Anat. u. Entw. Gesch. 23 1921

Halstedt W.S. J. exp. Med. 11 1909

Hoepke H. Strahlentherapie 93 1954

Mikroskopie 10 1955

Die Zellulartherapie Referatenblatt Frankfurt
1966 u. 1967

Fortschr. d. Med. 24 1968

Krebsgeschehen Jhrgg. 4 1972

Die wissensch. Grundlagen d. Zelltherapie
in: Zuwirkungsweise unspezifischer Heilver-
fahren

Hippokrates-Verlag Stuttgart 1972

Kidd and Toolan Amer. J. Path. 26 1950

Kment A. in Schmid und Stein Zellforschg. u. Zellulartherapie Huber Bern 1963

Landsberger A. Klin. Wochenschr. 40 1962 u.41 1963

Med. Welt 22 1963

Acta anat. 64 1966

Zelltherapie Frankfurt 34 1967

Mühlmann Erg. d. Anat. u. Entw. Gesch. 27 1925

MurphiJ.B. J. exp. Med. 24 1916

Niehans P. Das Alter Huber Bern 1936

Zellulartherapie Urban u. Schwarzenberg
München 1954

Die Zellulartherapie Frankfurt 32 1966

Weiss und Schüler zitiert nach Andres in Schmid u. Stein
Zellforschg. u. Zelltherapie Huber Bern 1963

Strehler B.L. Biologie des Alterns Aral Zeitschr. 1968

List of highly recommended books
for additional reading

Nutrition Against Disease by Roger J. Williams, Pitman Publishing Corporation.

The Stress of Life by Hans Selye, McGraw-Hill paperback.

Age Without Fear by Charles Degen, Exposition Press, Jericho, New York.

Nucleic Acid Therapy in Aging and Degenerative Disease by Benjamin S. Frank (Watch for the new edition in 1973.)

Biology, Observation and Concept by James F. Case and and Vernon E. Stiers, The Macmillan Company.

The Health Consequences of Smoking, U.S. Department of Health, Education and Welfare.

Magazines: *Prevention*, Rodale Press, Inc.

Free catalog of hundreds of your favorite books

Choose from hundreds of popular-priced books in your favorite categories and order them conveniently by mail. To receive your Pyramid Paperback Catalog, fill in the label below (use a ball point pen please) and mail to Pyramid...

PYRAMID PUBLICATIONS
Mail Order Department
9 Garden Street
Moonachie, New Jersey 07074

NAME_____

ADDRESS_____

CITY_____ STATE_____

P-4   ZIP_____